Twentieth Century in Prophecy

Elton R. Maas

VANTAGE PRESS
New York

All Bible quotations are from the King James Version.

FIRST EDITION

All rights reserved, including the right of
reproduction in whole or in part in any form.

Copyright © 1999 by Elton R. Maas

Published by Vantage Press, Inc.
516 West 34th Street, New York, New York 10001

Manufactured in the United States of America
ISBN: 0-533-12922-2

Library of Congress Catalog Card No.: 98-90802

0 9 8 7 6 5 4 3 2 1

To the Technocrats, who showed me what might have been—and even yet could be

Contents

Preface vii

I.	"Thy" Kingdom Came	1
II.	This and That	15
III.	The Stockholm Evidence of the Russell Tribunal	37
IV.	The Roskilde Evidence—Part 1	53
V.	The Roskilde Evidence—Part 2	75
VI.	Summary and Verdict of Sessions	103
VII.	Some Bible Prophecies and Events That Relate	129
VIII.	Equality	158
IX.	Indebtedness—Public and Private	175

Summary 181

Addendum 1: Guatemala 189
Addendum 2: Kosovo 191

Preface

There have been lots of treatises and books written on the prophecies of the Bible down through the ages. Some interpretations point the finger at Rome and the Roman Empire as the "bad guys" of the Revelation prophecies. Some elaborate on the Catholic Church as an evil force during the Middle Ages. Some, more recently, have concentrated on the Ezekiel prophecies as pertinent to our times, especially after the Soviet Union (USSR) became a powerful state. In the last context, I am thinking of Hal Lindsay's works.

It seems to me that tying the prophecies in with the observed and recorded events of our century should prove far more accurate than any earlier supposition that analysts have made. I hope to show the reader how America, Russia, the European nations, Karl Marx, Stalin, Lenin, and others were prophesied, and where they fit into the events of our century, according to Bible prophecy. None of them are called by the above names, but they are indicated by the descriptions and events that they have played a part in.

But before I get into the nitty-gritty of this, I feel I should tell you a little about myself. I am seventy-nine years old. I was a B-29 bomber pilot in World War II and participated in bombing a rail yard near Hiroshima on August 14, 1945. The squadron leader took us past Hiroshima after our bomb run, and I got a good look at the remains from high above. About forty-five minutes later, President Truman announced over the Armed Forces Radio that Japan had agreed to surrender. The war was over!

I had enlisted in the Army Air Corps, wanting to fly the biggest plane that we had and end the war. I think I came close.

Now I'd like to take you way back to World War I. In 1917 or early 1918, a young soldier training at Fort Riley near Manhattan, Kansas, where my family lived, came by to inquire if his parents could be put up for a few days while they visited him from their home in Iowa. While he was waiting for an answer, my dad came storming in in a bad mood, perhaps because he was being threatened with having his house painted yellow if he wouldn't buy any Liberty Bonds. He was a car dealer there in town, a businessman, but he was also only a second-generation American. His father had emigrated to that area of Kansas from Germany, and Dad didn't feel like supporting the French against his once-removed fatherland.

Anyhow, my five-year-old sister asked Dad if he didn't love her. He yelled back that he didn't love anybody. She started crying and the young soldier took her in his arms and told her he loved her. Elton Lowell's family did stay at our place while visiting him, and after they went back to Iowa, he kept coming to our home whenever he could get off and helped my mother by repairing things around the house when needed. When he left for overseas, nothing more was heard of him to my knowledge.

On the afternoon or early evening of Feb. 10, 1920, a young man came to our door and asked to see Mrs. Maas, my mother-to-be. My Aunt Clara answered the door and in answer to his request told him that Mrs. Maas couldn't see anyone that night. He went on his way. I was born about 9:30 that evening.

The next morning when my sister heard of the visitor, she supposed it must have been that young soldier, come to visit the family he had liked so much after returning safely from the war. She begged my parents to name me after him. Hence my given name, ELTON. The young man never returned, so one wonders if my sister was right or not. My middle name was given to me for my grandfather on my mother's side, ROBERT Fix, a soldier who served in the Civil War, fighting on the side of the North.

Years later, when I was in my mid-thirties I discovered my given name in an interesting place on the world map. It is the only place at the border of Europe and Asia in the Soviet Union on the Forty-ninth parallel. I eventually considered it significant in relation to potential crop yields in the Soviet Union in comparison to our own country. The Forty-ninth parallel in the USA is the border between Washington, Montana, North Dakota, etc., and Canada. Some 95 percent of the Soviet Union lies north of the parallel. There is a small town there and a small salt lake nearby, also named Elton.

Ten years later in the mid-1960s, I began browsing in the Cupertino Library, near where we lived at the time. I came across a small *Jewish Encyclopedia,* turned to the page "God, names of" and found at the bottom of the list: "Elyon, translated Most High, which was the Canaanite appellation for the supreme deity." It struck me as a spelling very close to my own given name. I later asked a Jewish talk-show host on KGO radio, Ira Blu, in San Francisco if my given name might be the modern spelling of Ancient Elyon, and he thought it might well be.

Getting back to how I acquired my given name, the episode with the young soldier, Elton Lowell, began just about the time of the "October Revolution" in Russia, or shortly thereafter. As I explain my reasoning on the prophecies relating to the twentieth century, you might begin to suppose that it was all set up by a higher power to stimulate me into certain paths of study over the years since.

In the Lutheran faith that I was brought up in, there is a practice of having a godmother and a godfather present at the baptism of the baby. Some six or eight years later, I was taken to visit my godmother, a Mrs. Godwin.

In or about 1920, my grandfather became too ill to take care of his farm near Alma, Kansas, where my dad and all his brothers and sisters were born and raised (four girls and five boys), and my dad and our family moved there from Manhattan to run the farm for the next five years, till my grandfather died, and Dad got his inheritance from the estate, and bought a farm of some five hundred acres about four and a half miles southeast of Manhattan.

During our five years near Alma, we attended church regularly, but the sermons were all in German, since there was a large German population in that area, so I didn't get much out of church service. As the expression goes, "It was all Greek to me."

However, when we attended church in Manhattan thereafter, the sermons were in English, and I began absorbing them with interest. Perhaps my greatest interest was the sermons on Daniel and his records. I was impressed by the protection of Daniel and his friends in the lions' den and the fiery furnace.

I was also impressed by Daniel's desire to know what the future would bring—so much so that a succession of angels were sent to explain things to him. How wonderful! Perhaps if I could build up that kind of strong desire and get the proper understanding—wouldn't that be great. This was even before I got into my teen years.

In the Lutheran faith, baptism occurs soon after birth, but it is considered not complete until the youngster confirms his faith in the early teens. I missed my confirmation at age thirteen due to the turmoil surrounding my mother's illness and death, soon after I graduated from eighth grade in 1933. I finally was confirmed the next spring at age fourteen.

While I was yet fourteen, in the tenth grade, the "spirit" or something moved me to ditch afternoon classes one day and go downtown to our public library and "browse." The title of a book caught my eye. It was *Looking Backward—2000 A.D. to 1887 A.D.* I checked it out, took it home, and read it from beginning to end. It was a beautiful adventure-love story about a man who allegedly was hypnotized by his doctor to help him sleep, in a sub-basement room. Apparently his house burned to the ground during the night, but the secret room was unaffected, and no one found him till 113 years later, when he was revived by the doctor who found him. The happy and beautiful society depicted in the story was a more up-to-date version of Sir Thomas More's *Utopia* and Plato's *Republic*. To me, it seemed like the potential fulfillment of that part of the Lord's Prayer we recited each Sunday in church: "Thy kingdom come, Thy will be done in (on) earth as it is in heaven." There was a sequel to that story by Edward Bellamy, called *Equality*, published about ten years after the first book. It is a continuation of the first story, and in the same conversational context. I finally acquired a copy of that later book when I was in my fifties.

In 1938 my father died and my oldest brother invited me to stay with him and finish high school in San Fernando, California, graduating in February 1939. Eventually I got a job at Douglas Aircraft Company, December 5, 1939, in Santa Monica, and I worked for them there and at the Long Beach plant until the fall of 1942. After Pearl Harbor, I took some classes in trigonometry at Los Angeles Evening High School to get ready to enlist in the Army Air Corps.

During recess one day, I heard another student in the class talking about something that perked up my ears. He gave me some booklets and magazines on "Technocracy." It sounded like something I had been looking for. Later, when I transferred to the Long Beach plant, I roomed and boarded right around the corner from a Technocracy section headquarters and joined the organization for the next six and a half years. A magazine, *Technocracy—A-21*, had a picture of a huge flying wing on the cover, allegedly capable of carrying fifty tons of bombs from our own shores and bombing Berlin, Rome, and Tokyo, and then returning nonstop to our own bases. So with that in mind, I vowed to become a pilot, to fly the biggest plane we would have, and end the war. I did fly in the biggest plane we had in World War II, and the war ended before we landed back on Tinian from our thirty-fifth and final mission.

In that same magazine with the flying wing on the cover was an article expressing a degree of sympathy for the Soviet Union and what it was suffering at the hands of Hitler and his minions after the invasion just four months earlier. If Russia was to fall, England would become just a few irrelevant islands off the coast of a Fascist Europe, subject to being conquered at Hitler's leisure, and America would need those flying-wing bombers to protect us. As it turned out, Russia fought the combined might of Western Europe to a standstill in 1942. By mid-1943, the Soviets were pushing the Wehrmacht back towards Berlin on all fronts, and the B-17s proved sufficient for our contribution to the bombing effort against Hitler. Another thought expressed in the A-21 article: there was so much sentiment in America against again becoming embroiled in Europe's battles that it would take a major catastrophe to make us unified against the Axis powers. Two months after that was published, we had that catastrophe—Pearl Harbor. The title of the article was "The Sellout of the Ages."

The "America First" movement, I discovered later, was formulated in the law offices of John Foster Dulles. It was a ploy of Hitler's to keep America out of the action. Allen Dulles was also a major contributor to the movement. John Foster became our Assistant Secretary of State under Truman, and Allen became head of the CIA for many years.

I went to boot camp in March of 1943, at Fresno, California, spent two months in Pre-pre-flight schooling at Washington State College in Pullman, took Pre-flight in Santa Ana, California, went to Tulare, California, for primary flight training in PT-17s, and while there, went to Bakersfield one weekend to visit some friends, Technocrats, who had moved there from Long Beach.

At a newsstand in Tulare, I brought a copy of a magazine called *Booktab*, with an article that caught my eye, "Stalin and God."

It told me that Stalin had been a seminary student at a Russian Orthodox Church School when he became attracted to the Communist movement. That's what impressed me. I wish I still had the article, but I lost it in my moving around from base to base.

By the fall of 1943, I was at Chico, doing basic flying in BT-13s. They had a "war room" on the base that I visited regularly. There was a map of the Eastern Front in Europe, and by that time, you could see the lines change weekly as Stalin's armies pushed Hitler's ever backward towards Germany. Each time I looked at the changes, I was thrilled at the success of our fightingest ally. It was 1959 before I found out from a *Population Reference Bureau* report just how costly in manpower the effort to protect themselves, and their nation, from Hitler's depredations really was. The report estimated that they lost 20 million military-age men in the battles. A recent television program on Russia's efforts—and losses—put the figure at 28 million dead at Hitler's hands, including those civilians who Hitler considered undesirable, especially Jews and Communists, in his death chambers that accompanied his armies.

Much of Russia was overrun and "scorched earth" by one army or the other. By comparison with the above, we lost less than half a million men in all theatres of combat, and little damage to our own land, other than what occurred at Pearl Harbor the first day. So, why did we turn against our staunch and fightingest ally of World War II, which suffered so much more than we did???

Now, to bring some of the foregoing into perspective, I heard, while in Technocracy, that the wife of Thorstein Veblen, an economist with a Ph.D. from Yale, read *Looking Backward* and insisted that her husband read it. The book apparently moved him a great deal, and he wrote several books that related to the setting up of such a society. *The Theory of the Leisure Class* and *Engineers and the Price System* were two of them, and were listed in the Technocracy Study Course bibliography.

My *Encyclopedia Americana* 1949 edition under "Social Reform Programs" since the first World War: "Technocracy" (vol. 25, pages 186c&d): "Its intellectual godfather was Thorstein Veblen, and some of the more active protagonists of the movement have been Howard Scott, Walter Rautenstrauch, Harold Loeb and Felix J. Fraser. It even attracted, temporarily, many of the leading industrialists and bankers when they were desperately grasping for a straw in the midst of the depression of 1930–33. The Roosevelt administration subsidized an elaborate investigation of American resources and plant equipment under the direction of Harold Loeb. Out of this grew two important books, *The Chart of Plenty* and *Potential Plant Product Capacity*.

In November 1941, *The Technocrat* magazine published the answer to a question from a reader: "One question I would like to have answered, is why don't we see more about Technocracy in the newspapers. Here we have an organization that claims to have the answer to the economic difficulties that are besetting the U.S. today—Is Technocracy being deliberately suppressed, or don't American editors recognize news when they see it?"

The answer is several pages long, but to cover the gist of it, on November 29, 1932, Manchester Boddy, editor of the *Illustrated Daily News*, introduced the subject of Technocracy to the public of Los Angeles. For the next month or so, Technocracy was front-page news. Throughout December and the first half of January, the *News* continued to run anywhere from half a page to a full page of Technocracy material each day. For lack of anything better, the *News* was running Edward Bellamy's *Looking Backward* as a daily serial, with a running comment comparing it with Technocracy's proposals.

On January 9, 1933, Mr. Boddy staged a debate with the celebrated liberal Lincoln Steffens at Los Angeles Philharmonic

Auditorium. The place was packed. "Resolved: Technocracy presents a basis for unlimited prosperity." Mr. Steffens defended the negative. Mr. Boddy appeared as the expert on Technocracy.

On January 13, 1933, Technocracy served notice that it did not intend to compromise with the Price System. At the Hotel Pierre in New York City, before an audience representing some $40 billion of capital, Howard Scott delivered an address on Technocracy explaining the place and effect of technology in the modern world. He served notice that Technocracy was prepared for a basic social change in which business, finance, and politics (the rich man's power over the nation's affairs) would have no place.

In December 1932, there were fifteen Technocracy stories in the *New York Times*, in January sixty-nine stories, in February only eleven, in March only one.

From January 23, 1933 to the next day, Mr. Boddy reversed himself completely on Technocracy.

And it was just about then that one Adolf Hitler gained enough financial support to attain control of Germany and form the Third Reich.

Some of the Bible students who read this will recall Jesus' remarks on how hard it would be for a rich man to enter the Kingdom of God (see Mark 10:17–27). More on Technocracy from my 1949 *Americana*: "The archaic Price System, said the Technocrats, prevented us from being able to distribute and use goods in anything like the highly efficient fashion that our mechanical plant enabled us to produce them." And "Whatever the future of Technocracy, it might be described as the only program of social and economic reconstruction which was in complete intellectual and technical accord with our age. It was far more up-to-date than Communism in the same way that the economic thinking of Veblen was more up-to-date than that of Marx. The remarkable progress of Soviet Russia was certainly due in part to its implicit adoption of a modified Technocracy, laying stress on production for service according to the latest technical processes, and reposing special confidence in engineers."

There are some twenty-five pages in that section relating to the many reform programs and movements over the past 2,000 to 2,500 years and how they have affected the poor, proletariat or working people, even quite a lot on the trade union movement. Many of these reformers may have been good Christians, thinking of Jesus' words in Luke 6:20:"Blessed be you poor, for yours is the kingdom of God," and endeavored to help the poor, but most were failures.

The Lord's Prayer taught us to want and pray for "Thy kingdom come, Thy will be done in earth as it is in heaven." In Daniel 2:44 there is promise of when this would occur—the question is what is that time frame? Is it in relation to the European Common Market nations as some interpreters of Prophecy would have us believe? Or has that time span already occurred in the past? Once that issue is settled, the prophecies neatly fall into place.

I. "Thy" Kingdom Came

Daniel 2:44: "And in the days of these kings shall the god of heaven set up a kingdom, which shall never be destroyed; and the kingdom shall not be left to other people, but it shall break in pieces and consume all these kingdoms, and it shall stand forever."

The preceding few paragraphs in Daniel refer to ten toes as nations that would not "cleave to one another" and would be "partly strong and partly broken." After Columbus discovered the Americas, or the islands of the same, Spain, Portugal, Great Britain, and France, and to a lesser degree Belgium and Holland, went forth and claimed property rights on the newly discovered territories. Later, as ships became more seaworthy and advanced, India, Southeast Asia, Australia, and the East Indies were likewise "colonized." During the early period of colonizing, Germany and Italy were a mixture of disconnected states, and it was much later when they tried their fortunes in the parts of Africa which Great Britain and others had not as yet "colonized."

In the meantime, many Europeans emigrated to the temperate regions of North America, and eventually they fought for independence from Great Britain in 1775–1781 and formed a new nation, the United States of America. At the time of the Revolutionary War, it may be estimated that only about 10 percent of what has since become the U.S.A. was in the hands of the European colonists. The rest was still in the control of the Native Indian tribes.

In Daniel 7, where we will find a most accurate indication of how these colonists would treat the native peoples where they appropriated land, as I'll pinpoint soon, there is an eleventh "little horn" that grows out of the fourth beast. The U.S. is primarily composed of European peoples, so I see it as the "little horn" that became more powerful than his fellows (Daniel 7:20).

In three places in Daniel 7, we see slightly different descriptions, but truly speaking of the same characters and events. Daniel 7:7: "It devoured, brake in pieces, and stamped the residue with the feet of it." Daniel 7:19: "which devoured, brake in pieces, and stamped the residue with his feet." Daniel 7:23: "and shall devour the whole earth, and shall tread it down, and break it in pieces."

The very fact of this being repeated three times in one chapter of Daniel is indicative of its utmost importance. I sincerely believe that no Common Market combine, or NATO nations' action could possibly, at some future time, accomplish what is described in the above events. Only the European colonial powers that actually did that over a period of some four hundred years, would fit the picture disclosed to Daniel.

As I remarked before, Great Britain lost its colonies in that part of North America which became the U.S.A. and Latin America gained independence from Spain, Portugal, etc. during the 1800s. Britain didn't lose India until after World War II. France lost Indochina in 1954, etc. Most of the colonies have gained their freedom since World War II, but the European emigrants who had settled there dominated the affairs, with little or no respect for the native peoples whom they displaced—even as in the United States. (Over a year ago, *Reader's Digest* published a book describing how the "Indians" of our land were treated. *Through Indian Eyes* is its title.)

Also there are two new names of characters introduced into the picture in Daniel 7: the "Ancient of Days" and "One like the Son of Man." There is also reference to an everlasting dominion/kingdom.

I'll be back to Daniel 7 later to elaborate more on the interaction of the "little horn" with the saints of the Most High, but first I need to make the connection to the Revelation 14 prophecy on these events.

Revelation 14:6:"And I saw another angel fly in the midst of heaven having the everlasting gospel to preach unto them that dwell on the earth, and to every nation, and kindred, and tongue and people." I interpret this to refer to a particular way of life, or economic system, or way a nation is to be run. In all reason it would take a lengthy period of time for the message of that angel to be spread around—worldwide—like from 1848 to 1917 in Russia (while the colonial empire systems still existed) and later on to China, Cuba, Indonesia, Latin America, etc. Karl Marx began his work in the mid-1840s and soon produced the *Communist Manifesto*, with his ultimate communist ideal: "from each according to his ability—to each according to his need," a theme taken almost literally from Acts 2:44–45, which tells how the early followers of Jesus shared: "all that believed were together, and had all things common, and sold their possessions and goods, and parted them to all men, as every man had need."

In Revelation 14:14–15:"And I looked, and behold a white cloud and upon the cloud one sat like unto the Son of Man, having on his head a golden crown, and in his hand a sharp sickle." Isn't that sickle a part of the Communist emblem? Continuing, "And another angel came out of the temple, crying with a loud voice to him that sat on the cloud. Thrust in thy sickle, and reap; for the time is come for thee to reap; for the harvest of the earth is ripe." Revelation 14:16:"And he that sat on the cloud thrust in his sickle on the earth and the earth was reaped."

Back to Daniel 7:13–14:"I saw in the night visions, and, behold, one like the Son of Man came with the clouds of heaven, and came to the Ancient of Days, and they brought him near before him, and there was given him dominion, and glory, and a kingdom—his dominion is an everlasting dominion."

To Revelation 14 again, 1–5:"And I looked, and, lo, a Lamb stood on the Mount Sion, and with him an hundred forty and four thousand, having his Father's name written in their foreheads. 4: These are they which follow the Lamb whither so ever he goeth. These were redeemed from among men, being the first fruits unto God and the Lamb. 5:And in their mouth was found no guile; for they are without fault before the throne of God."

Surely these 144,000 must be the saints of the Most High referred to in Daniel 7, which the "little horn" opposed.

Now to Revelation 17:12–14, we find more about the Lamb and those who follow Him: "And the ten horns which thou sawest are ten kings, which have received no kingdom as yet; but receive power as kings one hour with the beast, these have one mind, and shall give their power and strength unto the beast; These shall make war with the Lamb, and the Lamb shall overcome them, for he is Lord of lords, and King of kings; and they that are with him are called chosen and faithful."

Before we proceed further with telling who these characters are in our twentieth-century time frame, let's discuss the subject of reincarnation. There is a suggestion in three or four places in the Gospels that John the Baptist was indeed the reincarnation of Elias. I personally don't know if Elias is the New Testament spelling of Elijah or Elisha, but it doesn't really matter. The meaning is clearest in Matthew 17:12–13:"But I say unto you, that Elias is come already, and they knew him not. 13: Then the disciples understood that he spake unto them of John the Baptist."

Much of the work of Edgar Cayce, "The Sleeping Prophet," related to past lives of people who contacted him for readings. When questioned on the subject, he also referred to the Elias-John the Baptist references in the Gospels for biblical proof of the issue.

There is a book, *Conversations with God*, by Neale Donald Walsch (GP Putnam's Sons Publishing, New York), that at this writing (July 1997) is climbing the nonfiction best seller list (No. 3 last week). On page 204 it reads:

> Question: Is there such a thing as reincarnation? How many past lives have I had? Answer: It is difficult to believe there is still a question about this. I find it hard to imagine. There have been so many reports from thoroughly reliable sources of past life experiences. Some of these people have brought back strikingly detailed descriptions of events, and such completely verifiable data, to eliminate any possibility that they were making it up or contrived to somehow deceive researchers and loved ones. You have had 647 past lives, since you insist on being exact. This is your 648th.

On this subject, which I didn't mention in my preface, there is a study I came across and worked with for a while back in 1950. In the spring of 1950, *Astounding Science Fiction* magazine had a lead editorial by the editor, John Campbell, Jr., telling about the wonders of *Dianetics: The Modern Science of Mental Health*. I immediately sent for a copy from Hermitage House, the publisher, and when it came, I spent so much time reading it that my wife began complaining. I asked her "What do you want, a demonstration?" And she said yes. To make a long story short, I used the technique of putting her in "reverie" as per page 202 of the original book, until I saw her eyelids and eyelashes flicker, and five traumatic incidents were erased in about two and a half hours—the first demonstration session. The next day she called me at work about 1:00 P.M. and told me she had taken a nap a little while ago, and woke up feeling better than she had ever felt in her life. That sold me on the Dianetic techniques.

Dianetics soon hit the top of the best-seller list. I eventually sold my launderette business and took the first training course, held at the Los Angeles Coliseum.

Basically, *Dianetics* was a technique for releasing trauma, emotional and physical trauma, from the individual, and waking them up in moments of unconsciousness attendant to the trauma.

In the study it was known that late life emotional trauma often keyed in or restimulated painful trauma from earlier injuries—even, or especially, prenatal trauma (injuries to the infant in the womb) and form some kind of bond, the cause of many psychosomatic aches and pains.

Emotional trauma might be the death of a loved one, mother, father, sibling, friend, etc. One method of questioning for this type of emotional trauma was to have them go back to their last death, meaning the death of a loved one. In lots of instances, the "pre-clear" would go back to a time when he reported dying in a previous lifetime.

So *Dianetics* soon became the Church of Scientology and has since spread worldwide. Where *Dianetics* initially endeavored to clear up trauma in this current lifetime and create a Dianetic Clear, Scientology soon would work to release trauma from all past lifetimes, as necessary to attain ever higher potential for the individual. It was proven that IQ increased dramatically as trauma was removed from the body and/or psyche. I encountered several of these past-life incidents in "pre-clears" I worked with.

Needless to say, this gave me the clue to much of the prophecies relating to events here on the earth; how the Lamb and his 144,000 followers could be part of earthly events in our century. Reincarnation in infants at birth (that's when it occurs), with a subconscious urge or inclination to find and gravitate to the cause that they came down here to fulfill.

According to my 1949 *Americana*, page 292c, there were 115,000 Communist Party members in the Soviet Union in 1918. That sounds like a pretty fair percentage of the 144,000.

> The participants in this vocation of leadership were less politicians in the Western sense, than spiritually consecrated men and woman, dedicated to their cause with all the ardor of crusaders. The spirit, purpose and problems of this unique brotherhood are well suggested by Lenin's words to the 11th party congress in

1922; "Communist principles, excellent ideals, are written large on you, you are holy men, fit to go alive to paradise, but do you know your business?—we must learn to begin anew, again and again—In the masses of the people we are as a drop in the sea and we can govern only if we adequately express what the people feel—We shall not fall because we are not afraid to speak of our weakness, and will learn to overcome our weakness.

Now back to the Lamb and his followers: In my analysis, Revelation 17:12–14 clearly relates to events in Europe in World War II. Revelation 17:12:"And the ten horns which thou sawest are ten kings, which have received no kingdom as yet; but receive power as kings one hour with the beast. 13:These have one mind and shall give their power and strength unto the beast. 14:These shall make war with the Lamb, and the Lamb shall overcome them; for he is Lord of lords, and King of kings; and they that are with him are called chosen and faithful."

Every thought in this prophecy has relevance to the actual developments. During the 1930s there occurred the purge trials of Communist Party members and military leaders, ensuring that all left would be faithful to Stalin and the "party line." In 1940 Trotsky, who had had the most dissentive influence on Russian affairs since his ousting in 1927, was finally assassinated in Mexico City where he had moved. Thereafter, the Communist leadership and the people were solidly behind Stalin throughout the war, following Hitler's invasion in June, 1941.

Before Hitler's attack, Rudolf Hess, the number-two Nazi under Hitler, flew to Great Britain, with the purpose, I believe, of announcing Hitler's intentions of invading the USSR and inviting Churchill and Great Britain to join in the attack. Why else was Hess kept so completely incommunicado until his death just a few years ago? Churchill didn't agree to the proposal, but neither did he alert Stalin that the attack was coming. The belief on Hitler's part, that Great Britain might join with him in the attack, went back to 1918–1920 when Churchill was one of the prime movers behind the Western Intervention to overthrow the newly formed Bolshevik state.

The Russian Revolution effectively removed the power of wealth interests (the rich men) from the affairs of the new Soviet state. (Technocracy said real social changes had come to a section of our globe.) Eventually, when the first three 5-year plans had proved so successful in uplifting the well-being of the Soviet people, and the might of the Soviet state, the wealthy interests in the rest of Europe became troubled for fear that the same system would spread to their lands.

Hence, only token resistance was encountered by Hitler's armies as they proceeded to conquer and eventually control all of continental Europe. He had the use of all resources and manufacturing facilities, and he set up his own preferred leaders of those countries—Quislings, after the name of the one whom he installed in Norway. These are the kings who receive power for one hour with the beast.

About the dearth of resistance on the part of Europe when Hitler invaded. Technocracy called that phase a *sitzkrieg* war (sitting war) as opposed to the Blitzkrieg (lightning war) that was launched against the USSR.

Now the "Lord of lords and King of kings" term that refers to the Lamb, and the reverse order of these terms, emphasized in large letters in Revelation 19:16:Stalin commanded two positions of power. "Lord of lords" refers to his position as First Secretary of the Communist Party. His second position of power resided in his position of Premier of the Union of Soviet Socialist Republics, or "King of kings." Sometime after Hitler's attack, Stalin reversed the emphasis of his positions of power to more surely enlist the support of all the peoples of his realm for the effort against the invaders.

The intrigue on Hitler's behalf began as early as 1938, when Neville Chamberlain of Britain and Daladier of France met with

Hitler and Mussolini at Munich and agreed to the dismemberment of Czechoslovakia. The slogan was "peace in our time." That was what and when the Bible referred to with the words, "Peace, peace, when there is no peace. Then comes sudden destruction."

A book *Days of Our Years*, by Pierre Von Paassen, a Dutchman, carried a whole chapter on the evils and skullduggery of that Munich pact. The book topped the best seller list in this country in 1939 and 1940.

In 1946, a year after World War II was over, Technocracy sent a message entitled "Our Country Right or Wrong" to their membership analyzing the prewar developments and the postwar. They reported that documents of the Munich discussions stated quite openly that Hitler and Mussolini wanted Czechoslovakia dismembered so that Germany and Italy could attack the Soviet Union. Czechoslovakia, the last real ally of Russia, stood in the way, with formidable armored divisions and geographically natural defenses. So it wasn't peace in our time but rather a war of Fascist Europe on the Soviet Union, that France and England agreed to at Munich. It is no wonder that Russia was not invited to the conference.

Long ago, Technocracy defined Fascism as a consolidation of all the minor rackets into one major monopoly for the preservation of the status quo. Two of those terms need further definition: Business enterprises are considered minor rackets in Technocracy's opinion; the Status Quo means as things are—the virtually complete control over the affairs of man by the wealth interests of the time, through their contributions to political campaigns, through advertising in the media, (radio, television, newspapers, magazines, etc.) As for one major monopoly, every time you read of or hear of a corporate buyout, hostile takeover, merger, or other consolidation, that amounts to a step in the direction of Fascism.

Great Britain refused to join in with Hitler as his messenger, Rudolph Hess, wanted and subsequently suffered the consequences throughout the war; first bombers, then V-1 buzz bombs, and eventually V-2 bomb-rockets and forerunners of the modern intercontinental ballistic missiles. I have come to believe that Revelation 17:15–18 is about that phase of World War II as it affected London, England.

Revelation 17:15:"And he saith unto me, the waters which thou sawest, where the whore sitteth, are peoples, and multitudes, and nations and tongues; 16:And the ten horns which thou sawest upon the beast, these shall hate the whore, and make her desolate, and naked, and shall eat her flesh and burn her with fire; 17:for God hath put in their hearts to fulfill his will, and agree and give their kingdom unto the beast, until the words of God shall be fulfilled; 18:And the woman which thou sawest is that great city which reigneth over the kings of the earth'' (London?).

Great Britain still had a large colonial empire, which she controlled to a greater or lesser degree through World War II. India of Hindu beliefs, and Pakistan of Muslim beliefs became independent after the war. Recently, Hong Kong has been relinquished by the British Empire.

Returning to the Revelation 14:14–16 comment about the one like unto the Son of man who is told to reap the earth, with a sharp sickle in his hand, and he does, Daniel 7:13–14 has the same reference to one like the Son of man.

Daniel 7:14:"I saw in the night visions, and behold, *one like the Son of man* came with the clouds of heaven, and came to the Ancient of Days, and they brought him near before him. 14:And there was given him dominion and glory, and a kingdom, that all people, and nations, and languages, should serve him; his dominion is an everlasting dominion, which shall not pass away, and his kingdom that which shall not be destroyed.''

The above wording clearly indicates an earthly kingdom, not some ''rapture'' of the good people, and the subsequent interaction between the ''little horn'' and the Most High, and the saints of the Most High, and the people of the saints of the Most

High, indicates a generation or so before the matter is finally settled.

There were three (3) Axis powers of World War II: Germany, Italy, and Japan, which the United States had a major hand in finishing off. Daniel 7:24:"And he [the little horn] shall subdue three kings. 25:And he shall speak great words against the Most High, and shall wear out the saints of the Most High" (The cold war since 1945).

Harry Truman asked Stalin to send Molotov to the San Francisco conference for the formation of the United Nations organization. On April 22, 1945, Molotov stopped off in Washington to pay his country's respects to the new president. Truman began lambasting Molotov with the most vituperative "Missouri mule driver's" language that the others present were dumbfounded at. Never before had they heard of or witnessed such a tirade against a major representative of another country, our fightingest ally against Hitler & Co., before the war in Europe was finished. The cursing out was over the Russians' insistence that Poland have a Communist government, friendly to Moscow in control, rather than the Polish government-in-exile in London throughout the war. Russia had been invaded through Poland so many times—Napoleon, 1918–1920 Western intervention, and Hitler's attack in 1941—that Stalin felt it utterly important to have a friendly regime in Poland.

Two authors, D. F. Fleming of Vanderbilt University in *The Cold War and its Origins* and Fred Cook in *The Warfare State* both pointed out that date and event as the start of the Cold War. Exactly seventeen and a half years later was the Cuban Missile Crisis, when we might well have had to have a "rapture" to rescue or save enough live people to repopulate the earth in the event the crisis led to a nuclear holocaust—picked up by flying saucers, perhaps.

Daniel 7:25, continued: "and they shall be given into his (the little horn's) hand until a time, and times, and the dividing of time (3½ × 5 = 17½ years); 26:but the judgment shall sit. 27:And the kingdom and dominion, and the greatness of the kingdom under the whole heaven, shall be given to the people of the Saints of the Most High.''

You will find the best prophecy of the Cuban Missile Crisis in Mark 13:14–32. 14:"But when ye shall see the abomination of desolation, spoken of by Daniel the prophet, standing where it ought not (let him that readeth understand)—" Remember how our government was so concerned about those missiles being installed in Cuba, just ninety miles from Key West, Florida? That's the interpretation of them "standing where they ought not." 19:"for in those days shall be affliction, such as was not from the beginning of the creation which God created unto this time, neither shall be. 20:And except that the Lord had shortened these days, no flesh should be saved.''

In case you missed the significance of the Cuban Missile Crisis, October 22, 1962, you weren't alone. Jesus explains it in verse 32:"But of that day and that hour knoweth no man, no, not the angels which are in heaven, neither the Son, *but the Father*.''

In 1960, June or July, our San Jose paper that we were taking at the time reported that Russia then had 50,000 nuclear weapons—some of them as much as 3,000 times more powerful than the ones we dropped on Hiroshima and Nagasaki, I learned later—but never fear, we had 100,000 by then or twice as many as Russia, as if that would have made any difference in the net results, which would have destroyed all "flesh."

On September 22, 1960, about 5:00 A.M. I partially awoke and got what seemed to be a telepathic message, as if from a Flying Saucer commander, hovering overhead, that in two weeks we could be in a nuclear war.

I didn't find out what the danger had been until the *Reader's Digest* for April 1961, arrived with the lead article

"You Are Under Attack, The Strange Incident of October 5." That might have been the potential incident relating to "And except that the Lord had shortened those days, no flesh should be saved," or an earlier trigger to start the nuclear war that we have been all dreading for so long, before it could cause *total* destruction of all human life. Do you remember the movie *On the Beach*, where the radioactivity from the nuclear war had not reached Australia yet, but as it approached, all were going to take poison rather than suffer the debilitation of radiation sickness?

Back to the Cold War of the "little horn" against the saints of the Most High, Daniel 7:21–22:"I beheld and the same horn made war with the saints, and prevailed against them, 22:Until the Ancient of Days came, and judgment was given to the saints of the Most High, and the time came that the saints possessed the kingdom."

I will have to devote a whole chapter on the many aspects of the whole Cold War period, but before that, I heard an interesting "Final Jeopardy" answer on the program of Friday, February 21, 1997, relating to several eulogy remarks made by Winston Churchill about a British statesman who died in 1940, ending with calling him a man of great peace. The question was, "Who is Neville Chamberlain?"

I believe the name Church-ill is of great symbolism in relation to the "Christian" churches of our time, and their total failure to recognize the Kingdom of God that they have been praying for for nearly 2,000 years, which was foretold by Daniel more than 2,400 years ago.

Actually, there were at least two preachers who recognized the event, one a Leonhard Ragaz, a Swiss minister who confided his convictions to Pierre Von Paassen, as recorded in *Days of Our Years*, and the other a Reverend C. P. Bradley of Australia, who published a monthly newsletter *United People*, in the 1960s and 1970s.

But for the most part, the ill-churches have totally missed the boat, and instead they have found themselves repeating the most horrible lies and gross exaggerations that the "rich men" and their hirelings have manufactured to make everybody hate the Communists—who have striven so hard to fulfill God's will and purpose.

II. This and That

I have heard it remarked that the then Senator Harry Truman, when he heard of Hitler's attack upon the Soviet Union in June of 1941, expressed his true feelings—that we should stay out of it and let them kill each other off—and eventually help the losing side at an appropriate time.

I must have heard that before FDR was told to choose Truman over Henry Wallace for his vice-presidential running mate in 1944. At the time of the Democratic convention, I was part of a crew waiting for enough B-29s to be available so we could complete our training. I was really troubled by that decision, because I felt that Wallace was much more friendly towards our fighting ally.

The cussing out of Molotov on April 22, 1945 occurred two weeks before the German armies surrendered. With this indicative of how America would treat the USSR in the post-war era, after atom bombs were dropped on Hiroshima and Nagasaki, the Russian people had reason to believe that any day atom bombs might be falling on Moscow and other Soviet cities. After all, our nation was as capitalist and fearful of revolution as any European nation was in the 1930s. Then, too, the Marshall Plan aid to rebuild Western Europe and Japan, our World War II enemies, looked like a serious reversal of policy, threatening the USSR as much as Hitler did. They had to quickly develop their own nuclear arsenal, to protect themselves from the same "Rich Man's" efforts to do them in as Hitler failed to accomplish. In time, this literally "wore them out," as prophesied by Daniel 7:25:"And

Ten years later, in Johnson's War, we were hell-bent on getting still another quantity of our finest killed as we lost in Korea—and killing millions of "GOOKS," as our troops viewed the Vietnamese.

I leafleted the Republican Convention in San Francisco in 1964, refuting the lies that Barry Goldwater had publicized in the German magazine *Der Spiegel*, relating to his idea that Russia had broken lots of agreements with us over the years since the end of W.W.II. It was all a pack of deliberate lies. The *Congressional Record* that he refered to for proof did not support his allegations whatsoever.

In 1965 I prepared a lecture on Vietnam and our wrongful involvement there and gave it in several places: Merrit College in Oakland, San Jose City College, and Tantau Recreation Center in Cupertino, California. I marched in protest out to the port of Redwood City, from which napalm bombs were being shipped, with Senator Wayne Morse of Oregon, and thousands of others. I marched from downtown San Francisco out to Kezar Stadium with tens of thousands. I marched from downtown San Francisco to the Presidio with more thousands. I attended a lecture at Stanford University on Vietnam, given by Senator Frank Church of Idaho.

But before I proceed further with the Vietnam War analysis, I'd like to backtrack to the early 1800s, and a devout Bible student who interpreted a passage or two in Daniel as pointing to the year 1844 for a momentous event to take place. William Miller of Adventist fame expected the "rapture" of all the "good, saved" people to be lifted up to meet Christ in the air, and all the "bad, unsaved" to be destroyed, as also implied in Revelation 14:14–20, if one interprets the message that way. The Daniel 8:13–14 reference is that Miller saw as ending in 1844 is: 13:"Then I heard one saint speaking, and another saint said unto that certain saint which spake, How long shall be the vision concerning the daily sacrifice, and the transgression of desolation, to give both the sanctuary and the host to be trodden underfoot? 14:And he said unto me, *Unto two thousand three hundred days; then shall the sanctuary be cleansed."*

By that time most Bible scholars had come to understand that *days* in Daniel actually referred to *years* of real time. Miller assumed that the beginning of that 2,300 days was the same beginning as in the reference in Daniel 9:25:"Know therefore and understand, that from the going forth of the commandment to restore and build Jerusalem unto the Messiah the Prince shall be seven weeks and threescore and two weeks." This would constitute 483 years from the commandment in 457 B.C. till the day when Jesus was baptized by John the Baptist.

Needless to say, it was a grave disappointment for Miller and his followers, that what they had anticipated didn't happen. Something did indeed happen that decade, and perhaps began with Karl Marx striving on behalf of the Jewish people in Germany, to give them more liberty. In less than three more years, Marx and Frederick Engels prepared and published the *Communist Manifesto*, which was the first public declaration of International Socialism. Miller couldn't possibly have had any word on that event, which has had such an impact on world affairs since then, for it occurred far across the Atlantic Ocean in Brussels, Belgium.

In relation to this, I again refer you to Revelation 14:6:"And I saw another angel fly in the midst of heaven, having the everlasting gospel to preach unto them that dwell on the earth, and to every nation, and kindred, and tongue, and people." The "Gospel according to Marx" has indeed spread worldwide.

Somewhere in my readings of Jehovah's Witness books, I recall that the founder of that movement, I believe Judge Rutherford, foresaw the events of 1914 as leading to a grand event also. Of course it was towards the end of World War I that the Bolshevik Revolution occurred in Russia, as a direct consequence of the terrible conditions that the Russian people and their armies had been reduced to by the war.

To my knowledge, none of the Witnesses have ever recognized or appreciated the meaning of the Communist Revolution in Russia as the fulfillment of their expectations.

In the early 1960s, I likewise did some calculations on the meaning of Daniel 12:11–12, arriving at the conclusion that the 1,335 days pointed to the year 1966, but neither did I make a connection with an event that year until much later.

Daniel 12:11–12:"And from the time that the daily sacrifice shall be taken away, and the abomination that maketh desolate set up, there shall be a thousand two hundred and ninety days. 12:Blessed is he that waiteth and cometh to the thousand three hundred and five and thirty days.''

My interpretation was soundly based on my understanding of Mark 13:14 relating to the ''abomination of desolation standing where it ought not'' (the Cuban Missile Crisis of October 1962) ''spoken of by Daniel the prophet,'' yes, in Jesus' own words. Albert Einstein fretted a lot towards his end, that he might have destroyed the world with his theory of relativity and its potential results in the atomic age. Tracing back I found that Einstein received the recognition for his theory in 1921 while still one of Germany's chief scientists. Tracing back from 1921 to A.D. 631, I found that Muhammad had reached the peak of his career about then, and the Zoroastrian followers, who had retained the daily sacrifice in their rituals up till then, went over to the Islamic faith about then.

Well, what did happen in 1966 that Daniel's angel guide pinpointed? Perhaps the following circular, advertising the findings and evidence of Bertrand Russell's International War Crimes Tribunal.

Against the Crime of Silence

As the Vietnam conflict has developed and intensified over the past 4 years, many people have become aware of its wrongs, the "credibility gap," the ever mounting death toll—the *facts* of this undeclared war of might against the determination of a people for independence.

Some people have mounted, and participated in, massive demonstrations against the war. Some have tried to exercise some modifications through the political election process. Some have become so disenchanted with the whole establishment, and its unjust policies, that they are presently engaged in massive disruptive college demonstrations and strikes to effect some change in existing institutions and educational (indoctrination) policies. And some suggested an extensive "*Grand Jury Investigation*" of the Vietnam war to determine more exactly the details of what was, and still is, taking place far away in the steaming jungles, rice paddies and villages of South East Asia—and thereafter report to the world's people.

In mid-1966, Britisher Lord Bertrand Russell, a noted philosopher and long time "peacenik" (since approximately 1915) called for a new International War Crimes Tribunal to investigate the Vietnam War. Teams of investigators were sent out, and some sixty to seventy reports were returned and made to the tribunal meeting in session in Stockholm, Sweden, in early May 1967, and at Roskilde, Denmark, in late November 1967. Some of the findings of the Tribunal, based on the evidence presented, follow.

1. Has the government of the United States committed acts of aggression against Vietnam under terms of international law?
   YES (unanimously)

2. Has there been, and if so, on what scale, bombardment of purely civilian targets, for example, hospitals, schools, medical establishments, dams, etc.?
   YES (unanimously)

We find the government and armed forces of the United States are guilty of the deliberate, systematic and large scale bombardment of civilian targets, including civilian populations, dwellings, villages, dams, dikes, medical establishments, leper colonies, schools, churches, pagodas, historical and cultural monuments.

—Stockholm, 10 May, 1967
 Endorsed "ne variatur"
 The President of the Tribunal
 Jean-Paul Sartre

Have the armed forces of the United States used or experimented with weapons prohibited by the laws of war?
Yes, by unanimous vote

Have prisoners of war captured by the armed forces of the United States been subjected to treatment prohibited by the laws of war?
Yes, by unanimous vote

Have the armed forces of the United States subjected the civilian population to inhuman treatment prohibited by international law?
Yes, by unanimous vote

Is the United States Government guilty of **genocide** against the people of Vietnam?
Yes, by unanimous vote   (Roskilde, Denmark, December 1, 1967)

There is now a book, some 660 pages in length, *Against the Crime of Silence: Proceedings of the Russell International War Crimes Tribunal*, published by O'Hare Books, 1968, that thoroughly covers the reports to the tribunal—the evidence on which the above findings were based. Bertrand Russell, in his introduction to the volume, remarks:

This book, which records the work and findings of the International War Crimes Tribunal, should be studied thoroughly by anyone who is still in doubt about the role in Vietnam of the United States of America. It is a role which has been disbelieved often in the West, because it is in the nature of imperialism that citizens of the imperial power are always among the last to know—or care—about circumstances in the colonies. It is my belief, therefore, that it is in the United States that this book can have its most profound effect.

In these pages, in the evidence of Tribunal members and investigators, American military personnel and Vietnamese victims, are the facts about aggression and torture, anti-personnel weapons and aerial bombardment, the systematic destruction of civilians and their agriculture, hospitals, schools and homes.

From this evidence, it is clear that the United States has employed not only a huge army in Vietnam but tens of thousands of civilians at home in the harnessing of an advanced technology to the requirements of warfare in the Third World. It requires not only fiendish ingenuity but a vast industry to create and refine instruments of war to maim and terrify people, napalm which sticks more firmly to the human skin or canisters of steel pellets which enter and circulate in the bodies of their victims. These weapons and many others are dropped from aircraft which cost millions of dollars each. The Pentagon employs thousands of qualified specialists who are paid handsomely to advise on such questions as the effects of weapons on the human body or on vegetation, techniques of "Pacification" of foreign populations, how to compel prisoners to reveal information, how to administer poisons or destroy crops.

Why has the United States been making these efforts at such expense and on such a scale? The answer is no different in the case of America than in that of any other imperial power. The objects are domination, markets, cheap labor, raw materials, conscript armies and strategic points from which to control or threaten. If all of these factors do not apply to Vietnam itself, there is the certain knowledge in Washington that the example of a successful Vietnamese uprising will destroy the empire by destroying the myth of American invincibility. What can happen in Vietnam can be repeated, with local variations, in Thailand, Venezuela and the Congo. The interconnection of the U.S. Government and corporations is sufficiently documented—the United Fruit Company is only a particularly blatant example—for us to know the relationship between financial greed and military adventures. The American empire is a world system of exploitation backed by the greatest military power in history. In this role, America invokes the slogans of freedom and democracy, but when the system is challenged, as it has been in Vietnam, we see the reality behind the slogans and the reality involves war crimes. If this system is not checked, we face not only the continuing impoverishment of the Third World but also the consolidation of the American empire. Such a development would make the final confrontation with China and the Soviet Union the inevitable last step to world hegemony.

War crimes are the actions of powers whose arrogance leads them to believe that they are above the law. Might, they argue, is right. The world needs to establish and apply certain criteria in considering inhuman actions by great powers. These should not be the criteria convenient to the victor, as at Nuremberg, but those which enable private citizens to make compelling judgments on the injustices committed by any great power. It was my belief, in calling together the International War Crimes Tribunal, that we could do this, and this book is the record of the Tribunal's considerable success. It serves not only as an indictment of the United States by abundant documentation, but establishes the Tribunal as a model for future use.

This volume establishes beyond doubt the criminal nature of American actions in Vietnam. It is not enough, however, to identify the criminal. The United States must be isolated and rendered incapable of further crimes. I hope that America's remaining allies will be forced to desert the alliances which bind them together. I hope that the American people will repudiate resolutely the abject course on which their rulers have embarked. It is noteworthy that when there is revolt in the American ghettos, the

Pentagon operations room puts away its maps of Vietnam and proves itself incapable of directing more than one struggle at once. Finally, I hope that the peoples of the Third World will take heart from the example of the Vietnamese and join further in dismantling the American empire.

It is the attempt to create empires that produces war crimes because, as the Nazis also reminded us, empires are founded on a self-righteous and deep-rooted belief in racial superiority and a God-given mission. Once one believes colonial peoples to be *untermenschen*—"gooks" is the American term—one has destroyed the basis of all civilized conduct.

The following is an excerpt from a letter to the Executive Director of the Episcopal Peace Fellowship—from an American volunteer worker for the USAID (Agency of International Development) program for South Vietnam. "Can you imagine how my Vietnamese friend felt when an American soldier stopped me and asked, in a loud voice, 'You aren't a Gook, are you? Don't worry, my friend; we aren't killing *persons* over here, we are cleaning up the Gooks.' "

Perhaps the following satirical prose in the June '65 or '66 *Minority of One* covers the attitude. (Editor Arnoni was a Jewish internee in World War II)

THE DEVIL THEORY

In Vietnam the devil is everywhere,
   In the quiet hamlets on the countryside
      And even in Saigon.
The devil-killers, who go out
   To search and kill in devil territory
      Have it hard, for devils are everywhere
         And well-disguised as ordinary people.
   You have seen their faces in the news
      And read their stories.

A barmaid in Saigon,
    A laundress, quickly caught and shot,
        A little boy, the devil's son,
            Who sold his father for a candy bar,
Thirty children, murdered in a devil's school,
    Women and children, dead in a devil's shelter,
        A young man, dragged through a river to make him talk,
            An old man, remaining in a village after all have fled
A three-year-old, who gave away his father's hiding place,
    A girl, torn from her father as he was led away
        A Saigon professor who urged neutrality—exiled north.
And many more—you've seen the headlines;
    Six hundred devils killed today;
        They say it could take ten or twenty years
            To kill them all.
I find it strange
    That there are still so many devils to be found.
        Germans killed six million at Buchenwald,
            Auschwitz and other well-known sites
        But still the devil did not die.
Some foolish, crazy souls, sickened with so much death,
    Cry for respite, for an end to devil killing,
        But it must go on!
Millions of devils still survive
    In Vietnam, China, even here—
        In our State Department, churches, schools,
            Our town, perhaps next door.
There are hundreds of thousands, millions,
    Perhaps billions of devils.
        But no need to fear;
            We have the firepower
              To kill them all.
                  —Ruth Shapin

I want to quote some pages from the book *Against the Crime of Silence*, to give you some idea of the evidence on which the Tribunal's findings were based:

But before I do that, I would like to present you with the petition I prepared to be distributed during the big march out to Kezar Stadium in 1965—"Vietnam Perspectives."

> A call for a thorough <u>Grand Jury Investigation</u> of the issues of the Vietnam War—and every aspect, pro and con, of the East-West Cold War, which has thrown away <u>over a trillion dollars</u> in only 20 years.

Bertrand Russell may have had a copy when he decided the very next year to initiate his tribunal.

> The *Cold War* has now been with us for more than a generation, and shows many signs of reaching the boiling point where grave dangers loom for all mankind. Hundreds die every day in the little land of Vietnam, in an undeclared war of attrition.
>
> Within our own country, people are becoming quite energetic in their pros and cons of our government's foreign policies. Cries of "*War Criminal*" on the one hand and "*Treason*" on the other hand, call vivid attention to the rising temperature of the major factions that hold the spotlight of public attention.
>
> But name-calling does little or nothing to clarify the true issues and responsibilities which face our 20th century civilization. It does not begin to cover the background upon which decisions are made and objections are voiced. It is time that a thorough and objective investigation be made of all charges and counter-charges; all claims and counter-claims.
>
> A *Grand Jury Investigation* on behalf of the people of the United States, for their earliest possible education and assurance, is a prime necessity. It is imperative that the true facts and implications of the Cold War be determined and presented to the American people as completely and accurately as possible. It is essential that the members of this *Grand Jury* be carefully chosen, with

the utmost attention directed to their willingness and ability to remain unbiased and objective in their analysis—and unswerving in their assigned task of making publicly and widely known the conclusions of their findings.

In keeping with this goal of objectivity, it is essential that any individuals from the major factions of either side be prevented from composing the membership of the *Grand Jury,* but rather, people from all walks of life and who evidence a sincere desire to obtain the true facts and implications, should be chosen. In general, this will rule out the active politicians of the past 20 years of the two major political parties, and any they might conspire to select as well; for it is they who would be under investigation, and their policies, on the one hand, for their acceptance and promotion of America's Cold War policies. It is likewise essential that outspoken members of the opposition to our government's foreign policy be similarly kept from composing the membership of this *Grand Jury*.

On the other hand, it will be essential that both sides have *equal* opportunity to present their views, and the facts supporting their views, to the *Grand Jury* for their consideration. In pursuit of this goal, it will be desirable that everyone wishing to present additional facts and views be allowed and encouraged to do so; whether they be citizens or residents of our United States, or of some other country which has a need or desire to furnish evidence in the matter.

In order for the *Grand Jury* to be apprised of the relative import and judicial relevance of the various kinds and degrees of evidence and views, it is suggested that three men of experience in Judicial matters and factual evidence, with minimum bias, be chosen to preside over the *Grand Jury* throughout its program of accumulating evidence and presenting its findings to the American people.

Grand Juries are a tradition of the English speaking peoples which goes back many centuries. They are basically fact-finding bodies, with the authority to recommend corrective action. They have been used as preliminary procedure prior to indictment of criminals. They have been used as an investigative and propaganda device of the existing political and economic establishment, and/or various factions thereof. They have also been used as a "People's Panel," and thereby the only effective weapon against organized crime, *malfeasance in office, and corruption in high places.*

In keeping with the true spirit of the Grand Jury, yet considering that no state or federal law respecting the formation, selection and conduct of this particular Grand Jury will automatically apply; and considering that the actions and policies of our Federal Govt. itself are the subject of question in the matter, it is recommended that the number of *Grand Jurors* be raised to one above the current legal limit of 23—to 24, in addition to the three presiding officers before suggested.

This is a petition setting forth the goals and avowed intentions of primary purpose. It does not limit the further development and organization of such legal matters as are in accord with, and which might prove essential to, the progress and completion of the above stated goals, but rather encourages such as would prove necessary.

When the final conclusions are drawn, it might well be that there will evolve a majority opinion and a minority opinion, as presently often happens in many high level Judicial determinations. If the finding is against the formulators of American foreign policy, then the pattern of convictions and execution of justice against the Nazi Party of Germany and their leadership might will apply (and wouldn't it be far better for our own people to straighten things out than for us to have some overwhelmingly powerful outside agency exact punishment upon the whole nation)—but it will not be the express duty of the *Grand Jury* to do so; their duty only to bring the facts and conclusions out into the open for all Americans to freely examine, with the ultimate hope that they will indeed do what is right.

On the other hand, if the preponderance of evidence is against the Communists and their program, then dissension within our borders should automatically recede.

Following are some of the major charges and counter-charges, claims and counter-claims, which must be investigated and brought into perspective.

(1.) It is charged that Communism is a Cancer, a malignant intrusion on the world scene, which should be removed at all costs, even at the expense of the patient—civilization itself.

On the other hand, it is claimed that Communism is the new, and better, way of life, and that Socialism is the sure way for all mankind to advance into that better life while on this earth. <u>Let the Grand Jury determine the facts and truth of the matter to the best of its ability.</u>

(2.) In Vietnam, and in regards to the conflict there ensuing, it is charged that Communism is the aggressor, having infiltrated and engaged in active warfare against a sovereign state, which our nation has sworn to support.

On the other hand, it is charged that the United States, by its actions, is in direct violation of the United Nations Charter, the Geneva Agreements of 1954, and every moral and ethical code that this nation has ever indicated it would abide by. <u>Let the Grand Jury determine the facts and truth of the matter to the best of its ability.</u>

(3.) It is charged that Communism is a slave state type of existence, wherein everyone is subservient to the state and under a vile dictatorship; and that the United States foreign policies are directed toward preserving the freedom of peoples from such a slave existence.

On the other hand, it is claimed that in a Communist society there is far greater representation in government; that goals of such a government are primarily toward the benefit of all the peoples for long periods of time, rather than for the benefit of the wealthy minority which tends to control elections, choices during elections wherein the public has the lesser of two evils to choose from, as well as the general outcome of elections through the preponderant amounts of campaign funds, as in Capitalist nations. <u>Let the Grand Jury determine the facts and truth of the matter to the best of its ability</u>.

(4.) It is charged that the Communist system represents an atheistic, anti-Christ, movement against all belief in God or whatever He might wish.

On the other hand, it is suggested in some quarters that the Communist program for world control is the promised establishment of God's kingdom on earth, by the reincarnated "Saints," many of whom were martyred for the cause of Christ when their policies reflected pretty much the same as what the Communist goal consists of, and which was indicated by Acts 2:44–45; *"And all that believed were together, and had all things common, and sold their possessions and goods, and parted them to all men as every man had need."*—the Communist *goal "From each according to his ability; to each according to his needs."*—the "saints" having returned as foretold in Rev. 14 and Daniel 7:to reap the earth and set up an "everlasting kingdom." If the above be true, then the new song before the throne might well be, in truth, the Socialist system which prescribes compensation "to each according to his work" for a time, while progress toward abundant production is achieved, and with laws designed to prevent excess accumulation of wealth in the hands of a few. <u>Let the Grand Jury determine the facts and truth in the matter to the best of its ability.</u>

(5.) It is charged that the Communists are aggressors, and prevent the effective accomplishment of peace and disarmament by reason of their constant threat against the rest of the world.

On the other hand, it is pointed out that for thousands of years of history of private ownership there have been wars nearly all the time, in one place or another. It is further pointed out that the US is the nation whose economy depends upon an ever increasing warfare status in order to get rid of the tremendous production, keep the military-industrial complex happy, and prevent widespread depression conditions that prevailed during the 1930s. <u>Let the Grand Jury determine the facts and truth in the matter to the best of its ability.</u>

(6.) It is charged that the Communists lean toward military coups, overthrow by force and violence; and therefore are a threat to our way of life, and to our national security.

On the other hand, the Communists claim that they come into power only after the masses of the people are completely fed up with the way things have been run under the subtle (oft not so subtle) dictatorship of the wealth interests, and are overwhelmingly for the change. They next point to the military coups of elected governments, and subsequent military dictatorships set up, with the encouragement of the United States government, the CIA and other branches; in Spain, Guatemala, the Dominican Republic, Honduras, Brazil, Iran, etc., etc.; the many attempts to destroy Communism by military might in 1918–22 when some 7½ million Soviet people died as a result of the Western (democracies) intervention, Hitler's aggressive murder of over 20,000,000 more Soviet people (and encouraged to do so by all the major Western

Democracies in the Munich Pact of 1938); and emphasized that this is strong evidence of the shoe being on the wrong foot. <u>Let the Grand Jury determine the facts and truth of the matter to the best of its ability</u>.

(7.) It is charged that the Communists are confirmed liars—not to be believed under any circumstances, etc.

On the other hand, to quote a few of the prominent comments in the news regarding Vietnam:

"The American people are not being told the facts—they are being told what the Pentagon and the State Dept. want them to be told."
Senator Wayne Morse—3/2/65

Drew Pearson said—"We contend that we are in South Vietnam at the request of the popular government, to protect freedom. This is pure bunk. The government in South Vietnam has changed so often that no one can keep track—
St. Louis Post Dispatch—3/1/65

"The American people are not being told the truth about the clandestine war that is being carried out against North Vietnam. American reporters have been arrested by U.S. troops—and they have been denied access to news—this sort of totalitarian abuse never occurred in the blackest days of W.W.II."
Richard Starnes—*Rocky Mountain News*—3/19/65

U Thant, Sec. Gen. of the UN, said on Feb. 24, 1965; "The prospects for a peaceful settlement would become more and more remote with the passage of time—I am sure that the great American people, if only they know the true facts, and the background to the developments in South Vietnam, will agree with me that further bloodshed is unnecessary."

I suggest that a good look at the record (i.e., the U-2 incident, Bay of Pigs, the ups and downs of the disarmament talk and Dow Jones averages) and the U.S. official pronouncements on the same, would be pertinent to study in relation to such a charge.

(8.) It is suggested that no movement or group of people who de-emphasize God on the one hand, and emphasize the potential good in man (Soviet Humanism), could ever in any way be connected with God or the fulfillment of God's work or plans.

On the other hand, it is pointed out that there is widespread belief that all major religions are or were representative of God's messages to a limited group of people at one time or another, that they all encourage the ethical and moral, as well as spiritual, development of mankind—and yet at the same time, if God's kingdom were attempted to be set up under any one religious banner, that would automatically alienate all other religious groups and set them against the one so doing. Witness the Crusades, and India-Pakistan disputes, the "Inquisitions," etc.

But, by the "saints" emphasizing the improvement of man's lot on this earth, the potential good in man, and the golden rule or "Brotherhood of man," all can be drawn into the one "everlasting kingdom." What could be more logical—(with a cognizance of this probability now spreading panic in the ranks of the wealth interests)—and even if the Communists themselves won't come right out and admit the truth of it publicly?

If the wording of this petition seems to slightly favor the position of the Communist, perhaps that is essential, for the Grand Jury will indeed be composed of citizens of the United States, and therefore will automatically be to some degree patriotic towards our own country and the elected leadership—no matter how unbiased they might attempt to be. The slight leaning of this petition is necessary to offset that tendency. No one who is genuinely interested in determining the truth need object, since the stipulated goal is indeed truth and fact-finding of the very highest order possible.

We, the undersigned, do solemnly call for a thorough Grand Jury Investigation, a "People's Panel," of the issues of the Vietnam War; and of every aspect, pro and con, of the East-West Cold War which has been in progress for so many years. We further call for the fullness of knowledge on the matter to be publicly and widely known to all the American people, so that they might wisely and quickly set this country on the best possible course of action for the future of mankind.

Name (sign please) Address   Age

Bertrand Russell's Tribunal concentrated specifically on the actions of America's forces in Southeast Asia, of which I'll include some examples in the next chapter. He did hint at the underlying East-West conflict, and the empire-building efforts of the United States and its corporations to exploit the cheap labor and natural resources of the Third-World countries. He sincerely hoped that the Tribunal's findings would reach the American people and shame them into stopping the war; but the carnage continued with little pause for another six or more years.

The problem consisted of the news media of the U.S. and the government's ridiculing the efforts and findings of the Tribunal and/or effectively blanking out any mention of it in our media; just as they did with Technocracy in 1933; until the Mai Lai massacre hit the headlines in the early 1970s. Then for one day Russell was complimented for his efforts, but the next day the lid was clamped down tight on any further mention of it in the media.

Needless to say, the bulk of the petition I prepared in 1965 has not yet been addressed. As indicated in my petition, the American people need to investigate the matter, and also read the evidence that was denied them in the 1960s. So please proceed to the next chapter where I will present some samples of the evidence on each issue covered by the Tribunal.

III. The Stockholm Evidence of the Russell Tribunal

Following is some historical background on Vietnam. In the mid-nineteenth century, France invaded and claimed as a colony the Indo-China area, including Vietnam, Cambodia, and Laos. The Vietnamese people periodically fought the French to regain their independence. In his younger years, Ho Chi Minh went to France to study and became interested in Marxist and/or French Socialism. He returned to Vietnam and during World War II led the resistance movement against the Japanese occupation. After Hitler conquered France, the Vichy government and their representatives in Vietnam allowed Japan full control of that French colony, giving Japan huge stocks of foodstuffs for its armies. On March 9, 1945, Japan liquidated the French regime and substituted for it a protectorate led by Emperor Bao Dai. Elsewhere, I have seen a figure of 2 million Vietnamese killed or starved to death by Japan during the war years. The Tokyo War Crimes Tribunal charged Japan with war crimes in Vietnam. The president of the Tokyo Tribunal remarked several times that no matter what the relations had been between Vichy, the Free French, and Japan, the actions were to be regarded as crimes against humanity, and were to be treated as such by the Tribunal.

After Japan was defeated, Ho Chi Minh prepared a Declaration of Independence—patterned after our own 1776 Declaration against England. France soon recognized the government, but was back in Vietnam in 1946 in an attempt to regain complete sovereignty over the colony. The Vietnamese fought the French until 1954, till the French decided to agree to peace, after they were overcome at Dien Bien Phu, and the Geneva Accords were agreed to.

In November 1947, William Bullitt visited the Emperor Bao Dai in Hong Kong, where he had gone after the Japanese surrender. The "Bao Dai Solution" was American-inspired from the beginning. The Bao Dai government was formally recognized by Dean Acheson on February 7, 1950, as soon as it was set up. Important financial aid was given to France. Very soon, however, direct aid was given to the Bao Dai government by virtue of mutual security agreements between the United States and the Bao Dai, in December 1951.

The book *Against the Crime of Silence* goes on for seven more pages (71-78) detailing the ever-increasing escalation of American intervention from 1945–1964. On pages 116–117, several articles and amendments are quoted from the United Nations Charter that reflect on America's guilt in Vietnam; for did we not help prepare that charter and agree to it?

It reads in Article 1. "The purposes of the United Nations are: (1) to maintain international peace and security . . ." (2) "to develop friendly relations among nations based on respect for the principle of equal rights and self determination of peoples" . . . And Article 2, item 4, reads "All members shall refrain in their international relations from the threat or use of force against the territorial integrity or political independence of any state, or in any other manner inconsistent with the purposes of the United Nations."

Item 12 of the Final Declaration of the Geneva Conference in July 1954 states: "In their relations with Cambodia, Laos and Vietnam, each member of the Geneva Conference undertakes to respect the sovereignty, the independence, the unity and the territorial integrity of the above-mentioned States, and to refrain from any interference in their internal affairs."

The Declaration on the Granting of Independence to Colonial Countries and People, adopted on December 14, 1960 at the UN General Assembly, states in part:

(The General Assembly)... Convinced that all peoples have an inalienable right to complete freedom, the exercise of their sovereignty and the integrity of their national territory, solemnly proclaims the necessity of bringing to a speedy and unconditional end colonialism in all its forms and manifestations; and to this end declares that:

1. The subjection of peoples to alien subjugation, domination and exploitation constitutes a denial of fundamental human rights, contrary to the Charter of the United Nations and is an impediment to the promotion of world peace and cooperation.
2. All peoples have the right to self-determination; by virtue of that right they freely determine their political status and freely pursue economic, social and cultural development.
3. Inadequacy of political, economic, social or educational preparedness should never serve as a pretest for delaying independence.
4. All armed action or repressive measures of all kinds directed against dependent peoples shall cease in order to enable them to exercise peacefully and freely their right to complete independence, and the integrity of their national territory shall be respected.
5. Any attempt aimed at the partial or total disruption of the national unity and the territorial integrity of a country is incompatible with the purposes and principles of the Charter of the United Nations.
6. All States shall observe faithfully and strictly the provisions of the charter of the United Nations, the Universal Declaration of Human Rights and the present

Declaration on the basis of equality, non-interference in the internal affairs of all States, and respect for the sovereign rights of all peoples and their territorial integrity.

Returning to history for a moment, on December 2, 1823, President Monroe, in his annual message to Congress, declared a new policy: (1) The United States would not interfere in the internal affairs of or the wars between European powers. (We set this aside twice this century; in World War I on the side of France and England; and in World War II following Japan's attack on Pearl Harbor.) (2) The United States recognized and would not interfere with existing colonies and dependencies in the Western Hemisphere. (3) The Western Hemisphere was closed to future colonization (or recolonization), and (4) Any attempt by a European power to oppress or control any nation in the Western Hemisphere would be viewed as a hostile act against the United States. Some thirty years later, this policy began to be called the **Monroe Doctrine**.

On March 12, 1947, President Truman called together a joint session of Congress and asked for a $300 million appropriation to halt the advance of Communism in the world. The money was to be spent in Greece and Turkey to help promote a government to our liking—and against the E.L.A.S. who had led the resistance against Hitler's occupation. The E.L.A.S. was Communist leaning, and the side that we supported had collaborated with Hitler. Thus was established a new doctrine to our foreign affairs—*The Truman Doctrine*. Our country, then and since, has adhered to that doctrine as much as possible. (We couldn't stop the Communist takeover in China—it was too big a chore even for us, but that had a great influence over our subsequent policy on Vietnam, the domino theory, you know.)

Elsewhere, through our CIA-conducted operations on behalf of, and monetary assistance to, in many instances, outright dictators (as long as they abided by our wishes), many areas of the world have been prevented from going Communist, or were overthrown before they could go that direction. One example, is in the late 1960s when Suharto and the military overthrew the Sukarno government in Indonesia. I heard that a million "Communist" supporters of Sukarno were killed by the military in the process, all at the instigation of our government and its CIA operatives.

Considering what I called to your attention in the first chapter of this book, the *Truman Doctrine* was a declaration of war against the "Everlasting Gospel," which indeed has spread worldwide and to many "nations, and kindred and tongues and peoples," and against the Kingdom of God foretold by Daniel 2:44.

Consider that we have "in God we trust" on our currency, and we installed not too long ago a new phrase in our Pledge of Allegiance, "One nation, under God." Is that not the supreme blasphemy???

The Bertrand Russell Tribunal did indeed find the United States guilty of aggression against the nation of Vietnam; and guilty of violating the 1954 Geneva Accords on Vietnam in many serious areas—and thereby caused the death of some 6 million Vietnamese by the end of hostilities in the early 1970s in the process.

From 1945 to the early 1970s, America supported five different factions, or puppet regimes of our making, in Vietnam; the French through Marshall Plan aid, and then for four or more years some 70 percent of the French budget for their war of suppression against the Viet Minh armies. The Bao Dai government from 1950 onwards, and Diem, whom the U.S. had Bao Dai appoint as his prime minister, who followed orders from the U.S. to ignore the Geneva Accords, in fact violated them in many important parts. Then, in 1963, Diem was eliminated and Khan became our puppet. Later Ky replaced Khan.

Five presidents and their administrations were involved in the murder of Vietnamese: Truman, Eisenhower, Kennedy, Johnson, and Nixon. In December 1953, then–Vice President Nixon said, "It is impossible to put down our arms before victory is complete." Isn't it appropriate that he had to eat those words twenty years later as president???

Now to some of the reports on the second item of the verdict: "We find the government and armed forces of the United States are guilty of the deliberate, systematic and large scale bombardment of civilian targets, including civilian populations, dwellings, villages, dams, dikes, medical establishments, leper colonies, schools, churches, pagodas, historical and cultural establishments."

There are some 160 pages of reports, testimony of individuals and teams, that were sent by the Tribunal into Vietnam and Cambodia to investigate what was going on, firsthand. Thirty-two separate reports relate to the charges and weapons used against villages and people, churches and pagodas, hospitals and schools, etc.

Several reports relate to the Cambodian area. Bernard Couret, a French journalist, says,

> It is a well known fact that Cambodia has never threatened anyone, but it has been proved that the Saigon Government, working with the Americans, has for years been trying to overthrow the neutralist regime established by Prince Sihanouk.
>
> Although, up to the present, not one frontier violation by military material or by armed Cambodian units has been recorded, violations of Cambodian territory by land, sea and air recorded between 1 January, 1961, and December 21, 1961 totaled 1,608. In 1965 there were 621; in 1966 1,332, and there were 1,395 by the end of October 1967. These violations caused the death of more than 200 persons, approximately 400 wounded, and gave rise to the destruction of whole villages.

I remember reading in our newspaper in the early 1960s how a number of Buddhist Monks (Bonzes) had set themselves afire in a dramatic protest against the treatment of the Khmer people in Vietnam. Little or nothing was told of what they were protesting. The book goes into detail on the subject.

Finally, there is the problem of the Bonzes. Approximately, 3,600 of them are refugees in Cambodia. Their exodus began in 1961. Many of them told me of their persecution by the Saigon authorities; their schools had been closed since 1961–1962, making Buddhist studies impossible—the exodus has become widespread since the bombing of pagodas began in 1964.

[Khmers are an ethnic minority in Vietnam. They are of Cambodian origin, but live throughout most countries of Indochina.]

The interviewee was the Bonze Superior;
Q. Can you give details of the suppression by the US–South Vietnamese authorities, of the culture, customs and traditions of the Khmer minority of South Vietnam?
A. Yes. They have closed all the Khmer schools, they have forbidden the population to learn the Khmer language—the policy began to be applied from 1960–61 onwards. The suppression of the Khmer culture has become more and more rigorous all the time and is increasing even today.

In the schools the children have been forced to learn the Vietnamese language. All the Khmers have been forced to change their names. People were summoned to the district office and there they had to choose Vietnamese names, which were written up in the district registers.

Q. When did you arrive here and why did you leave your village?
A. At the beginning of the year 1961, the US-Saigon forces surrounded the pagoda where I was chief Bonze. The Charek Pagoda; they arrested all the Bonzes and the congregation there; they bound their hands and carried them away. Fortunately I was not there. I had been invited to ceremonies in another village. The authorities interrogated the Bonzes to

find out where the Chief Bonze was. They explained that I was absent. They forced the other Bonzes and members of the congregation to come with them to find me. On the way the American Saigonese forces killed two of the members–the others fled with their hands still tied.

Witness, Chou Uon, 55 years old:

Q. Why did you come here and when?
A. I came in 1966—the planes came and bombed our village and raked it with machine gun fire. Everything was destroyed, burnt. I fled with my wife. She was killed. I was wounded in my eye by a bomb fragment. (His left eye was destroyed and there was a large swelling on the left side of the eye.)

Q. When did you arrive?
A. At the end of December 1966.

Q. Was there much damage in the village?
A. It was completely destroyed.

Q. How many dead and wounded?
A. Thousands, mainly old people, women and children.

Witness, Chou Hong, 50 years old.

Q. When did you come and why?
A. I came two days ago. There were a lot of people in my village because all the villages around had been bombed and the people fled to our village. Five days ago the Americans came and attacked our village. They bombed with artillery and planes. Many people were killed, and also buffalo and other animals.

Q. What do you think—why was your village bombed?
A. It is their policy of extermination against our people.

Q. Did they try to make you change your religion?
A. Yes, they wanted us to become Catholics.

Questioning of a Khmer mercenary, Muong Ponn, 39 years old.

Q. How long have you been in the army?
A. I have been in the army 19 years. At first I was in the infantry battalion of the French army of the Far East. When the French left they handed me over to the South Vietnamese government. I have been in the intervention forces since 1957. I am a master sergeant.

Q. What were the functions of your unit?
A. It was to carry out "mopping up" operations in the villages.

Q. What is meant by mopping up?
A. We were dropped by helicopters; we fired at everything and killed everyone.

Q. Who gave the orders to do that?
A. The Americans.

Q. Can you describe a recent operation against a Khmer village?
A. Yes, on the 12th of April this year, 1967, we took part in an operation against a village at Phum Oc Yum. First of all the 105s bombed it. Then we were dropped by parachute. There was a terrible massacre, mostly women and children. There were only a few men, apart from the very old ones. Our instructions were to shoot at everything that moved.

Q. Did Americans take part?
A. Yes, the commanding officer in charge was an American.

Q. What kind of village was it?
A. It was almost entirely Khmer. It was after this operation I decided to leave.

At the time of these investigations some 20,000 people from Vietnam were refugees in Cambodia.

And now to some reports from North Vietnam.

The general destruction of health institutions up until Feb. 1967, was 95, with nearly all the technical equipment also damaged or destroyed. There were 87 administrators, nurses and doctors killed; and 35 wounded. Of the patients, 262 were killed, 246 wounded, and 65 civilians in the near vicinity were also killed.

For instance, that of the Leprosourim of Quyn Lap—It consisted of 160 buildings and could care for up to 2600 patients. In the last 5 years, more than 5000 lepers had been cared for, and more than 1000 of them had been sent home as cured.

The first attack was June 12, 1965, at 8PM. Numerous American planes flew over and dropped hundreds of bombs and rockets on the Leprosourim; they came back several times to drop more bombs. In these raids, 139 patients were killed, 9 doctors and members of the staff were killed and 100 other persons were wounded. Through Oct. 1966 the Leprosourim was bombed 39 times.

In Appendix A of the book *Against the Crime of Silence*, there is a list of all the hospitals and other medical establishments that were bombed and the dates of the raids: February 1965, 5 raids; March, 8 raids; April, 7 raids; May, 7 raids; June, 28 raids; July, 19 raids; August, 23 raids; September, 11 raids; October, 11 raids; November, 7 raids; December, 3 raids (129 bombing and strafing raids in 1965 on medical facilities).

1966, February, 5 raids; March, 8 raids; April, 11 raids; May, 11 raids; June, 8 raids; July, 3 raids; September, 3 raids; October, 2 raids.

Some hospitals were repeatedly bombed: hospital of Quang Binh province, 11 times; hospital of Ha Tinh province, 17 times; hospital of Huong Khe district, 8 times, hospital of Ky Anh district, 5 times in two days, August, 15–16, 1965.

Attacks Against Educational Establishments:

Attacks began on August 5, 1964, with the bombing of the primary school of Suag Giang, in the province of Ha Tinh. In the afternoon a second raid was directed against the secondary school of Hon Gai situated on a hill top. It is important to be aware that these air raids which began on the above date have taken place in a country where since 1954 the effort to stamp out illiteracy and build schools has been remarkable. In the ten years between 1954 and 1964, 95 percent of North Vietnam's population has become literate. The number of students in schools of general studies reached 3,000,000 with 60,000 in secondary school where the lower and middle grade professional workers are educated. On the university level, the number of students rose from 500 in 1954 to 50,000 now, in 1967.

According to the Commission of Inquiry of the Democratic Republic of Vietnam there have been a total of 391 schools destroyed in North Vietnam. The schools attacked and bombed are to be found in nearly every part and province of North Vietnam.

Let us cite a few examples. Two day-nurseries inspected by the fourth Inquiry Commission, the first at Vinh, had been razed to the ground and only the steps remained. As it had been evacuated, there were no victims. The nursery—in the province of Thanh Hoa—had been bombed to the ground on January 29, 1967. Nine of the ten children who were living there and three of the staff were killed.

Other examples must be emphasized, in particular, the bombing of the secondary school at Hong Phue in the province of Ha Tinh on Feb. 9, 1966, at precisely 16:30 hours. The children rushed to get to the slit trenches but the bombs fell directly on them, hollowed out large craters and caused a heavy death toll. Thirty-three children perished as a result of this attack.

On January 20, 1967, while we were in North Vietnam, the school of Tan Thanh in the province of Ninh Binh was attacked from the air at 12:45. A single plane flying in from the sea released an air-to-ground missile. This missile came right into the classroom killing the teacher while he was actually writing on the blackboard. Another teacher and five children who were on a bench near the school and twelve students 6 to 8 years old were killed and seven others wounded.

Places of Worship Destroyed by American Bombing:

Since 1965, according to Vietnamese sources, there have been more than eighty churches and thirty pagodas attacked and destroyed from the air. Priests and monks were killed in these attacks.

A specific example: the church of Kien Trung, situated near Phat Diem, was attacked on April 4, 1966 at 18:20, precisely at the time of Sunday Vespers. The church was full of worshippers and the result was catastrophic; seventy-two dead, thirty-six males and thirty-six females of whom 34 were children. There were forty-six wounded.

Near the church, the school and a dispensary were also destroyed. We collected direct evidence from eye witnesses, and we examined the wounded at the site. In particular, we saw the family of Mr. Trong whose father and four children were killed. We saw the family of Mr. Loi, of which two parents and four children were killed. And there remains only a daughter, who at the time of the attack, was in the marketplace. We saw a child who was wounded on the way to the church; she has had both legs amputated as a result. We saw a Mr. Tunc, of whose family ten were killed and two were wounded. Only the father is still alive. The family of Mr. Phong now consists of only one child of 8 years old; two parents and two children were killed. Finally we saw young Thang, who now has only one arm; he is five years old and his mother died in the attack on the church.

A statement by US pilot Charles Tanner, whom the Team interviewed in Hanoi, demonstrated further that US bombings of nonmilitary targets are pre-calculated and organized.

According to his statement, which we have submitted to the Tribunal in a recorded tape, Lt. Commander Tanner unequivocally states that the order of attack was to 'first destroy dwellings by bombs, then burn out shelters by napalm, and then kill or wound with CBUs all the people who would be driven out of their shelters by the napalm.' His formation made successive sorties with these three types of weapons.

These facts, together with the other evidence, clearly delineate the realities of the bombing of the north by the US. The manner in which the US is waging air war against Vietnam constitutes not only bombing against targets of a non-military nature, but also criminal acts with the calculated aim of massacring the civilian population.

The CBUs (canister or Cluster Bomb Unit) carry about 640 small grenade-size bomblets that a timing device separates the container casing at an altitude of about 800 meters. The 640 guava bomblets are flung out and follow a parabolic trajectory and are distributed over the objective in an elliptical pattern about 1 kilometer long by about 500 meters wide. Into the casing are cast 260 to 300 steel balls 5.56 mm in diameter. Strictly an antipeople weapon. On REAL TV May 22, 1997, you may have seen the demonstration of a CBU being dropped from a plane, and the scattering of the bomblets.

And now to the bombing of dikes in Vietnam; but first a report on the destruction of dikes in Holland in 1944–45. Perhaps you know from history books that Holland reclaimed hundreds of thousands of acres from the North Sea hundreds of years ago. There was even a story about a small boy who spotted a leak and made a hero of himself by plugging the hole until someone came along to help. Anyhow, the Tribunal book includes a report on how serious it was to destroy dikes.

> During the final months of the Second World War the Nazis exposed the Dutch civilian population to a form of war crime the United States and British Governments especially designated as

crimes against Humanity. To prevent the advance of Anglo-American troops, the German High Commissioner in Holland, Seyss-Inquart, opened the dikes and by the end of 1944 flooded approximately 500,000 acres of land—the barbarism of Seyss-Inquart in destroying dikes and starving civilians made him appear in the eyes of the Western officers as "one of the worst war criminals"–Of the 185 Nazis indicted at Nuremberg only 24 were sentenced to death, Seyss-Inquart was one of the 24. His crime was considered to be one of the most monstrous of the Second World War, and prominent among the charges against him at Nuremberg.

Some facts on Bombing of Dikes:

The bombs used for the destruction of dikes were of about 1500kg, and combined with the use of ball (CBU) bombs. If the destruction of dikes alone was intended, then demolition bombs would have sufficed; but ball bombs, the exclusive purpose of which is to kill and wound men and beasts, were used in combination. Further, after destroying dikes by bombing, additional bombing was conducted against people engaged in repair work. The dike at Traly, Thai Binh province was bombed twice in 1967 while it was under repair; 52 bombs were dropped and 32 people were wounded. In Quang Binh province, the tidewater control dike was bombed several times, destroying paddy fields of 1500 hectares. According to our investigation, the bombing by US is so accurate that it is inconceivable for places which have no target other than dikes to be bombed by chance. It should therefore be judged that the US forces have carried on bombing purposely to destroy dikes and kill and wound the people repairing them.

US bombings and strafing of the entire dike network were exceptionally violent and concentrated in the months of July, Aug., and Sept. of 1966, when the water level was very high. The following number of raids against the dike system had taken place: From Feb. to June 1966, 55 air raids; in July 1966, 69 raids; in Aug. and Sept. 1966, 136 raids.

I have given the reader just a few of the many reports and analyses found in 312 pages in the first half of the book reporting what was covered at the session in Stockholm; May 2 to 10, 1967. The findings of guilt did not deter the American forces whatsoever, as evidenced in a report by wire from Hanoi on the 19th of November, 1967.

> On the 17th of November, the American imperialists once again committed extremely grave crimes against the Vietnamese people.
> They launched violent attacks against several residential districts and in the center and in the suburbs of the capital, Hanoi, and in other provinces of North Vietnam. In attacking the capital Hanoi three times, at 7:15, 9:00 and at 10:55, they mobilized planes of the US Navy and the US Air Force, which made 76 attacks, dropped 56 explosive bombs, more than 30 of them being delayed action bombs, 12 containers containing 200 ball bombs, including delayed action ball bombs, fired 50 fragmentation missiles, thereby killing 33 civilians and wounding 158 more, and destroying numerous dwellings and property belonging to the people.

It goes on listing the districts hit, the hospitals hit, the schools hit, and the area of the International Control Commission where "Assistant Officer Mangal Chand, 25 years old, of the Indian delegation, was killed by a missile fragment, and another member of the Indian delegation was wounded."

About the Tonkin Gulf incidents that brought about the House-Senate Tonkin Gulf resolution, there were three incidents reported in our newspapers. The first occurred close in to the North Vietnam coast, and may have been for real. The second incident allegedly lasted several hours, as if there were a running battle going on, and has always been denied as having been participated in by North forces. The third incident belied any reality to the second incident. A "blip" showed up on the destroyer's radar screen; one salvo from the destroyer, the blip was gone—no more action.

There was a political military conference in Hawaii two months before the Tonkin Gulf incidents. The Tribunal figured that the whole scheme was planned or concocted there to get Congressional approval for the subsequent resolution.

Shortly after the Tonkin Gulf incidents, the *Nation* magazine published a lengthy article on the falsity of the second incident—which by itself was used by President Johnson to get Congressional approval to do the extensive bombing of North Vietnam, which I have elaborated on at length earlier in this chapter.

IV. The Roskilde Evidence—Part 1

The second session of the International War Crimes Tribunal was held at Roskilde, Denmark. The proceedings began on November 20th and terminated on December 1st, 1967.

Since the end of the Stockholm session on the tenth of May, 1967, the war not only continued, but escalated in intensity. More American troops arrived in Vietnam; Hanoi and Haiphong were being subjected daily to a massive bombardment. By this time more bombs had been dropped on Vietnam than had been used in the whole Pacific Theatre of Operations during World War Two. Before the end of 1968, at this rate, it became certain that bomb tonnage dropped on North and South Vietnam would exceed tonnage dropped in all Theaters—Europe and Pacific—in World War Two. The larger proportion of these bombs continued to be the murderous CBUs, which the Stockholm Tribunal Session had forced the Pentagon to admit were being massively used. It was evident that the civilian population of this tiny country was enduring carnage.

At the ripe old age of ninety-five, Bertrand Russell made this opening statement to the Second Tribunal Session:

As we meet in quiet comfort, the people of Vietnam are made to suffer new and greater crimes. Hour by hour, day by day, the horror intensifies, inflicting wanton pain and torment upon a nation which has known no peace. We are calm and unhurried. We have carried on our work these many months in the tranquillity of our laboratories and reading rooms. We have studied the war through the means which are customary to us as scholars. The written word, pictorial evidence, the material remains of incinerated villages—all these are transported to us for examination at our convenience. We form our judgment as we would judge right or wrong in a war of antiquity. The anguish of the Vietnamese people is as remote from our lives as that of a people who are removed from us by centuries.

We have not shared their suffering. Our judgment does not vindicate them, but vindicates ourselves. The idle man has no right of judgment over those who support the concepts of morality and justice by their active struggles against cruelty and injustice. Our words are a small charity, causing us to endure no hardships. Ours is a meager role in history. Can we consider ourselves actors when the drama of our epoch is a life and death struggle between the peasants of Vietnam and the mechanized slaughter perpetrated from Washington?

The course of history is being shaped in Vietnam. We shall not alter it much by our words. It is the people of Vietnam who refuse to submit to United States hegemony who are altering history. They are proving the might of men inspired by ideals. They face the richest armies and the most modern instruments of extermination. America spends seventy million dollars per day to enact mass murder, but the impoverished nation of Vietnam cannot be deterred. The power of this example will be felt in every continent where the poor have been cowed before the military prowess of their oppressors. The power of their example extends even to the affluent nations of the West, where their heroism has stirred politically inert peoples to massive protest against the new barbarism of the Pentagon. What we may say counts for little beside their deeds. By examining and exposing American war crimes in Vietnam, we do no more than ask to be counted on the side of those who are struggling in a just cause. By fulfilling the minimal obligations which we recognize, we seek merely to avoid moral impotence.

We have already presented conclusive evidence of the aggressive character of the United States intervention in Vietnam.

As we proceed, we must recognize how profoundly the concept of aggression covers all America's crimes in Vietnam. We are not examining a border dispute between Great Powers to determine which is the aggressor, in the sense of the first party to transgress the frontiers of another. In such a case, I should be reluctant to say that the incident of aggression would constitute the totality of all war crimes in the ensuing battles. I do not agree with the rigorous adherence to formal definitions which prevented our placing the bombardment of Hiroshima and Nagasaki on the same moral plane as the crimes of the Axis in World War II. Japan's aggression does not exonerate the United States for using the atomic bomb against civilian centers. But I believe firmly that America's aggression in Vietnam is a pure crime of conquest, delineating precisely between aggressor and victim. I cannot remember any way within my own lifetime in which the term 'naked aggression' so profoundly explained the full meaning of the bloodshed.

In Vietnam there is a race of men who, in modern times, have never been free and who have never known peace. This explains why the war knows no middle course between national salvation and genocide. Men who have known only war, injustice and suffering can make no compromise, for they possess nothing to concede. They may lose their lives, but these were already taken from them. Their culture may be brought to ruin, but it was already perverted and abased by the power of alien forces. Their wealth may be wasted, but it was already stolen. A century of Western oppression forms the prelude to a quarter century of violent strife. The struggle aims not to restore the past, but to create the future. The epic struggle of Vietnam continues so long as one man survives, embodying these hopes, demanding to create a new life, free of impoverishment and fear, with dignity and courage. Every man of this race, who has not been bought by the United States, carries this hope. Each threatens America; for each must be exterminated if America's will is to prevail.

We meet in the coming days to consider the extent to which America is already guilty of genocide, in the most exact juridical sense of the term. America's intent is plain; the logic is unmistakable. Our task is to hear the evidence, document the atrocities, and declare the extent to which this—the most heinous of crimes—has been committed.

Vietnam has much in common with other struggles for justice. Although it is not the task of our Tribunal to consider these other struggles, we cannot forget them. They are the raison d'être of the new tribunals and future inquires. By our modest effort, we wish to affirm the duty of those who have sought only to contribute to civilization to stand with the men and women who struggle to uphold its values. Let this remind the complacent that the crimes against the American Negro will also receive the most exhaustive examination. Let this warn the arrogant spokesmen of the 'American Century'' that the crimes against the people of Latin America will also be exposed.

We are not judges. We are witnesses. Our task is to make mankind bear witness to these terrible crimes and to unite humanity on the side of justice in Vietnam.

—Bertrand Russell, November 1967

Opening Address to the Second Session by Jean Paul Sartre:

So the second session has begun. I would remind you that we have three principal accusations to consider:

Have the American Forces used or experimented with new weapons, or weapons forbidden by the laws of war, such as gas, special chemicals, etc.?

Have Vietnamese prisoners been subjected to inhumane treatment, in particular, torture or mutilation, forbidden by the laws of war?

Have there been unjustified reprisals against the civilian population, in particular, execution of hostages? And have camps for forced-labor been created, populations deported, or other acts committed which contribute to the annihilation of the population and which can be legally characterized as acts of genocide?

Before proceeding further with the evidence contained in the second half of *Against the Crime of Silence*, I need to again refer you to the Daniel 7:and 12:prophecies. Daniel 7:24:"and another shall arise after them; and he shall be diverse from the first, and he shall subdue three kings." (There were three Axis powers in World War II. America was involved in subduing all three.) 25:"And he shall speak great words against the most High, and shall wear out the saints of the most High, and think to change times and laws; and they shall be given into his hand until a time, times and the dividing of time [$3\frac{1}{2}$ times]." If one thinks of a time in relation to the five-year plans that the Soviet Union used to develop their economy and defense preparedness, then $3\frac{1}{2}$ times would add up to $17\frac{1}{2}$ years—the exact time span from the start of the Cold War, April 22, 1945, to the Cuban Missile Crisis on October 22, 1962—so I have long known the time implication of the prophecy. Not till just recently did I finally comprehend the meaning of *Changing Laws*.

In Daniel 12:5–7, there is again reference to $3\frac{1}{2}$ times, which I'll remark on later. The point I make is that I have known the meaning and relevance of times, but not the *laws* referred to until recently.

The Russell Tribunal makes extensive reference to the "Laws of War," which the evidence shows were massively, indiscriminately, and brutally violated by the American forces and their puppets and allies in the Vietnam War.

> The principles posed by the Convention of the Hague are very important. The Preamble of Convention No. IV respecting the Laws and Customs of War on Land—18th of October, 1907, states:
>
> Until a more complete code of the laws of war has been issued, the High Contracting Parties deem it expedient to declare that, in cases not included in the Regulations adopted by them, the inhabitants and the belligerents remain under the protection

and the rule of the principles of the law of nations, as they result from the usages established among civilized peoples, from the laws of humanity, and from the dictates of the public conscience." Article 22:"The right of belligerents to adopt means of injuring the enemy is not unlimited."

Article 23:"In addition to the prohibitions provided by special Conventions, it is especially forbidden: To employ arms, projectiles, or material calculated to cause unnecessary suffering."

Article 25:"The attack or bombardment by whatever means of towns, villages, dwellings, or buildings which are undefended is prohibited."

Article 27:"In sieges and bombardments all necessary measures must be taken to spare, as far as possible, buildings dedicated to religion, art, science, or charitable purposes, historic monuments, hospitals, and places where the sick and wounded are collected, provided they are not being used at the time for military purposes."

Following World War I, new rules of warfare from the air had to be developed. The governments participated in the Washington Conference, that met at The Hague from December 1922 to February 1923, "allowed the bombing of military forces, military establishments and factories engaged in war productions; but forbade aerial bombardment for the purpose of terrorizing the civilian population. The general principle followed was that air attacks are legitimate only when directed at a military objective."

The questions had also been examined by the League of Nations: The Assembly of September 30, 1938, for example, "considering that new consecration had to be given to these principles, recognizes the following principles as a necessary basis for any subsequent regulation: 1) The intentional bombardment of civilian populations is contrary to Law; 2) The objectives aimed at from the air must constitute legitimate military objectives, and must be identifiable; 3) Any attack on legitimate military targets must be carried out in such a way that the civilian population in the vicinity not be bombed through negligence."

These general principles were repeated in Article 6 of the Statute of the International Military Tribunal at Nuremberg: Article 6.

> The following acts, or any of them, are crimes coming within the jurisdiction of the Tribunal for which there shall be individual responsibility; b) War Crimes, namely violations of the laws and customs of war. Such violations shall include, but not to be limited to, murder, ill-treatment or deportation to slave labor or for any other purpose of civilian population of or in occupied territory, murder or ill-treatment of prisoners of war or persons on the seas, killing hostages, plunder of public or private property, wanton destruction of cities, towns or villages, or devastation not justified by military necessity. Article 18: Civilian hospitals organized to give care to the wounded and sick, the infirm and maternity cases, may in no circumstances be the object of attack, but shall at all times be respected and protected by the parties to the conflict.

Actually, the Allies began violating some laws of war in World War II, with the fire-bombing of Dresden, Germany, creating a raging inferno that did devastating fire damage.

I was on a 500-plus B-29 raid on Tokyo, May 23, 1945, with napalm and magnesium incendiaries, which recon photos later showed burned to ashes 15 to 25 square miles of the heart of Tokyo. It was defended, however, as our plane alone had ten or more flack (shrapnel) holes in the skin of our plane. The excuse from higher command was that nearly all Japanese households did some phase of defense production right in their homes.

Perhaps that philosophy carried over to the Vietnam war—with the bombing of every village, school, hospital, church, pagoda, etc., in North Vietnam.

On the use of new weapons in Vietnam, there were the CBUs used against civilians, children, people heading for shelter, or forced out of their shelters by napalm, and dike repair crews, and first aid people trying to care for the injured.

There was the practice of throwing tear gas grenades into tunnels in South Vietnam where people had sought shelter—and the concentration of the gas in the confined space would be so severe that many would die of asphyxiation before they could get out to fresh air, mostly women and children.

It was common practice for soldiers to file a notch in their bullets, thus creating a dum-dum bullet in effect. Dum-dum bullets had been outlawed for a long time. Then came along the M-16 rifle that caused a tumbling effect to the bullet as it entered the human body—which was even more damaging than the dum-dum bullets.

Last but not least, there was the ever-increasing use of herbicides against the food (rice) crops of the Vietnamese, as well as the jungle and forests of the country. Agent Orange, which so severely affected our own troops for years afterwards, just from handling and dispensing the stuff, had not as yet been developed and used yet in 1967.

Before proceeding further with the evidence, I need to say that I have agonized for months on just how much or how little of the 660 pages of the Proceedings of the Russell International War Crimes Tribunal should be called to your attention in this book. I feel sure that every person in the world should study it thoroughly. But, after all, it is past history, some will say. But isn't that the central theme of this book, the history of the twentieth century as foretold by the prophecies of the Bible???

Bertrand Russell's efforts were supposed to settle the matter according to Daniel 7, for Russell clearly fits the description of the "Ancient of Days." I'm looking at a picture of him at the Tribunal's Organizational meeting in London. Daniel 7:9:"The hair of his head like pure wool." He was ninety-four years old at the time. The picture is on page 656 of the volume.

Surely the Vietnam War was the most dastardly, horrifying, bloody episode in America's foreign policy since World War II. And yet it is only one of many murderous actions of our government (yes, yours and mine) that have occurred over most of this century; and that news media, controlled by the rich man and his hirelings, have failed miserably to keep the people aware of our actions (is that a free press?)—or distorted the issues by accusing the "enemy" (The Kingdom of God) through all sorts of exaggerations and "red herrings."

As early as 1965, reports out of Vietnam indicated that U.S. forces were using two kinds of gasses to attack Vietcong hiding places—CS- and CN-labeled tear gasses.

A sergeant in a weapons platoon was asked the difference between CS and CN. He said that CN was stronger—it makes you feel nauseous; it makes you feel like your stomach is coming up.

U.S. officials have emphatically denied the use of any nausea-causing agent in the gasses.

The official view that the use of such gasses was permissible under codes of warfare was challenged by Senator Wayne Morse, Democrat of Oregon, an international lawyer and vigorous critic of the administration's Vietnam policies.

Morse said he was sure that gasses inducing nausea were among those that the United States, as well as other nations, had in the past described as "justly condemned by the general opinion of the civilized world."

"It is interesting to see," Senator Morse said, "how easy it is, once we depart from the principles of international law, to violate more and more of them."

At one time, the use of gas in South Vietnam released a wave of indignation throughout the world. Washington then promised to prohibit the use of toxic gasses, but the prohibition was of short duration. In fact, in the course of the raid made on

September 5, 1965 against the village Vinh Quang, province of Binh Dinh, a battalion of Marines under the command of Lt. Colonel Leon Utter flooded the civilians taking refuge in air raid shelters with 48 containers of poison gas, killing 35 and wounding 19 (26 women and 28 children).

There are several pages listing other villages that were subjected to the same kind of gas attacks, and the results on the civilian population.

The use of weed killers, defoliants, herbicides, etc., is a form of chemical warfare, as used in Vietnam. Never before had the subject of their use to destroy the food supply of an enemy population been the subject of laws of war. Perhaps they had not been developed sufficiently before the end of World War II to be seriously considered.

The closest thing to the crop destruction in Vietnam was the orders and opening of the dikes in Holland towards the end of World War II by the German High Commissioner in Holland, flooding some 500,000 acres with sea water and threatening widespread starvation of the Dutch people. Seyss-Inquart was tried and sentenced to death at Nuremberg for this most serious war crime.

So shouldn't the vast destruction of the Vietnamese food crops and poisoning the land for years into the future constitute just as great a war crime—if not even a greater one???

Alexander Minkowski, Professor of Pediatrics, Paris Faculty of Medicine, has some enlightening remarks in his report on the above use of defoliants:

"—I would like to stress the consequences of defoliations."

I think that it's obvious that a product which, at the start, is meant simply to make the leaves of a tree fall is not per se noxious. However, it seems that in the long run, and on a long term basis, this might be one of the most dangerous and terrible forms of biochemical warfare. In principle, the aim of defoliation is to destroy the cover of the land and therefore to make troops easier for airplanes to see. Another of its aims is to starve those who are fighting.

But it was very quickly realized that these weapons, when they are used on a large scale, are toxic for the population, and particularly for the children. These products destroy the food supply, and among the populations which are famine struck, the children are the weakest and the first to fall.

I will conclude with a short personal comment. It is my belief that this war, which is a particularly terrible one, uses products of this type because in this way it is possible to reassure American public opinion and assuage the conscience of the average American, whereas in actuality we are tending toward one of the most devastatingly imaginable forms of chemical warfare.

Some statistics on page 329 on herbicide use: "1961—the spraying of weed-killer in 6 provinces—500 hectares of crops destroyed (2.47 acres = 1 hectare), 1962—12 provinces sprayed; 11,030 hectares destroyed. And the latest figure we have of 1966—32 provinces sprayed; 876,490 hectares of crops destroyed." Think for a minute; that amounts to over 2,165,000 acres of crops destroyed, or more than four times the 500,000 acres flooded in Holland by the Germans, in 1966, and the defoliants contaminated the land for future production as much or more than the salt water contamination of the Dutch farmland.

David Kenneth Tuck, a former Specialist Fourth Class with the Twenty-fifth Infantry Division from January 8, 1966 to February 9, 1967, voluntarily traveled to Roskilde to testify at the Tribunal on what he saw and experienced in Vietnam. He hadn't read the 1954 Geneva Accord on Vietnam until he got back to the States.

Tuck reported seeing a sergeant behead a wounded enemy soldier and throw the head down the hill in the direction where others might be lurking—to let them know we meant business.

He reported seeing an interrogation where the enemy soldier had a knife pried under his toe nails, the soles of his feet, and under the eyeballs. Then when he still hadn't talked, he was put in a barbed-wire cage on his knees, with the barbs so close that if he moved the barbs would press into his flesh—for two days.

Tuck reported seeing another bound enemy prisoner thrown from a helicopter from several thousand feet up.

He said it was standard policy in his outfit not to take any prisoners, and he was told by the officers not to take any prisoners unless it was a North Vietnamese officer, who would instead be sent up to a higher echelon to be interrogated.

Mr. Tuck was asked further about this. His answer: "Well in the first place, I would like to say that the enemy prisoners were never left to die by themselves; they were always executed, but they were never left to die of their wounds. I have also seen other cases in which a wounded prisoner was laying there supposedly waiting for an evacuation helicopter, and I have seen several GIs just go over and shoot him in the head just to be done with it."

Without any special orders? "No, well, in some cases they had orders, and in other cases, since it was standard policy in my outfit not to take any prisoners, that is what we did. If a man was not an officer and he was wounded, we just got rid of him. This happened all the time in Vietnam, it is a common thing."

Tuck also told about assaulting a village. If shots were fired towards the assault troops, they would have a "mad minute" in which everyone would cut loose, with tanks, machine guns, rifles, etc., for about one minute at the village before proceeding further. He says this "mad minute" was common practice. He saw it happen numerous times.

It was standard operating policy when in Viet Cong controlled country to surround a village and go in and assemble the inhabitants in a bunch in the center of the village. All young men who looked as if they were able to bear arms were sent away in helicopters to be interrogated by the South Vietnamese. The women and children were sent to a refugee camp (strategic hamlet, new life hamlet, concentration camp). Sometimes everything in the village would be burned.

Mr. Tuck was asked about the refugee camps; what were the conditions of life inside them?

> Most of the refugee camps that I saw were invariably near a Special Forces camp. From what I could see from these people they looked just like they were starving; they were in rags. Shortly after we got over there I was on a work detail to dump some garbage into a sump, which is a hole dug in the ground for that purpose. As soon as we had dumped this, these refugees—a whole lot, a horde of children, it seemed—literally jumped into the sump and fought like animals for the garbage. The refugees—I got the impression from what I saw—were left to eke out their own living. A lot of the women in the refugee camp had to turn to prostitution to earn a living.

Mr. Tuck was asked about the use of gas into tunnels.

> It was frequently when we were on an operation we would find a lot of tunnels, and a lot of times we did not know whether there were VC in there or not. So what we would do, we would have to use tear gas to bring them out. A lot of times it would be women and children besides the VC in there. But most—but often again a lot of times it would only be women and children. The tear gas does not kill anyone as long as they can get out to the fresh air.

Another soldier, Peter Martinsen, traveled to Roskilde to testify on his tour of duty in Vietnam as a prisoner interrogator, and what he did and observed. He was there from September 1966 to June 1967. He said, "I cannot think of an interrogation that I saw in Vietnam during which a war crime, as defined by the (1949) Geneva conventions, was not committed."

Martinsen said that the field telephone, "wired" to various parts of the prisoner's body, and cranked, produced severe shocks. He said that it was standard equipment of the interrogator. The first time a lieutenant applied the shocks to a prisoner's sexual organs, he had to turn away. He could not watch it. He told of a case where a captain was "wiring" a prisoner when the prisoner died of "heart failure."

He did hundreds of interrogations during his tour. He tells of one time he tried something different. He ordered a prisoner to dig his own grave, threatening him the whole time with a rifle pointed at him. Before he finished digging, the prisoner broke down and cried.

As for wounded prisoners:

> It was the policy to see if the prisoner would talk first before he was treated; and then the treatment could be withheld as a promise; you will be treated if you do talk but you certainly will not be treated if you don't talk. This was a method of interrogation.
>
> There were some people in a tunnel, and the Americans found the tunnel entrance. They looked inside the tunnel and found it was occupied. They immediately gassed the tunnel with tear gas. It might have been "antiriot" gas. Then they proceeded to chase the people from the tunnel. The tunnel was so long (10 miles) they chased the people for 24 hours, until the people came out the other end of the tunnel very badly gassed and coughing. All of them sounded as if they had serious damage to their lungs. The prisoners were brought to us, and I only looked once. Four of five of the prisoners were girls between the ages of 16 and 20. They were nurses and laborers. The girls were brought to us in very bad physical condition. They were coughing, wheezing, and gasping, as if they had—very bad asthmatic attacks. I took one look and called for the doctor. The doctor gave them all injections and dosages of adrenaline. The prisoner compound was nothing but a tent with barbed wire around it. The prisoners were not segregated by sex as the Geneva Convention calls for. The prisoners were not given proper bedding. The girls were lying on the

ground, which was rather damp, and one (17-year-old) girl grew more ill. It was the policy that all prisoners must be interrogated. I kept calling the doctor to say, "Doctor, she has pneumonia," I knew that because I have had pneumonia. The doctor kept saying, "No, no. She'll get better!" and she kept getting worse. She was finally evacuated to the First Division field hospital, where I hear she died. I denounced the stupidity of the doctors and the stupidity of the commanders for trying to keep her there to interrogate her, and I almost got court-martialed for it. That was one of the most odious things I saw there.

Another soldier, Master Sergeant Donald Duncan, made the trip to Roskilde to be questioned and testify on his experience in Vietnam. The questions and his testimony cover some fifty-six pages. I'll summarize as much as I can.

Mr. Duncan was born in Toronto, Canada, in 1930. He became a naturalized citizen of the U.S. in 1955, while in the U.S. Army at Fort Riley, near Junction City, Kansas (about thirty miles from where I grew up near Manhattan, Kansas). He spent three years in Europe where he first came across Special Forces. He was trained for Special Forces in 1960–61 (when the Bay of Pigs effort was made—Special Forces from Fort Bragg, North Carolina, were involved in the training of the invasion force). He moved into training the new recruits in Special Forces. The recruits had to have at least a sergeant's rating to qualify.

Some of his instruction was on the subject of interrogation of prisoners. The instructor had to "pussy-foot" around the issue of whether they were being taught to torture, execute prisoners, etc. The catch phrase was, "If I told you to do that, the Mothers of America would not approve."

When he got back from Vietnam, he authored a book *The New Legions*—the hard truth on Vietnam, on the military practices there and on the foreign policy that has made more enemies than friends for the Americans.

Mr. Duncan was questioned and elaborated on an incident from his book: "It took place after a battle; there was—what we would call a fire fight, both sides shooting, etc. The strike force was pinned down in a rather open area; airplanes were called in. You couldn't actually call this a hamlet, it was maybe a collection of twenty huts, twenty-five huts perhaps, many of which were destroyed; it was recognized that there would be many civilians in that village—(we get a relative problem here: Who is it better to have killed, a few civilians that we don't know, or us?)

After the fire fight stopped, the strike force went into the village. Those houses that were still left standing were searched; all material taken out of them that had any value at all, souvenirs mostly; and then the houses were put to the torch. In the process of this, of course, as you might fully understand, the people who owned the houses weren't too happy to see their houses burned, and in a couple of cases they protested to the soldiers and were beaten, and in fact one woman was shot by one of the soldiers. And finally, one prisoner was brought forward with a broken leg. He was tied with what we call communication wire. It's a very thin wire with a plastic coating and with a steel-wire core in it and it bites very deeply into the flesh. His arms were tied twice; once at the biceps and once at the wrists, behind his back. He was dragged into the center of the village.

First of all he was interrogated by what would be called the executive officer of the strike force, without any results. When I say interrogated, I mean that questions were shouted and screamed at him, while simultaneously one of the other soldiers was kicking the broken leg to the point where the bone finally was pushed through the flesh. During this interrogation a lieutenant had a knife in his hand (a type of knife called a "Kabar" an item that is issued in the United States Marines, very popular with Special Force in Vietnam and a treasured item amongst strike forces) and he was teasing the prisoner with the knife; drawing—not actually cutting—but scraping with the point, tracing marks on his chest and stomach. As time went on, of course, the prisoner was not speaking, and finally the prisoner was literally pinned to the ground with this Kabar knife. The knife was pushed straight through his stomach. (It has a blade about 9 inches long.) Then another platoon leader jumped on the prisoner, who was now almost in a state of shock, and he proceeded again to attack him with a knife, only this time ripping the stomach cavity open and going into the cavity and extracting the gall bladder, which he treasured as a trophy. As a matter of fact some three weeks later he was still wearing the gall bladder around his neck in a little plastic bag as a good luck token.

Knowing that the interrogator usually met with little success even after much torture of the prisoner, I can imagine that that gallbladder bag might have been used to intimidate future prisoners, and at an opportune time the bag pulled out and the conversation gone something like this; "See this? This is a gallbladder that used to belong to a 'gook' who stubbornly refused to answer my questions. You have one too. So start talking—fast!"—or words to that effect in Vietnamese.

When I was in the service, we were informed that all we had to divulge if captured was our name, rank, and serial number.

I suppose if you are fighting for Democracy (private business) and God is on your side ("one nation under God") (the God of Corporate Enterprise, merchants and the rich men), then you can totally ignore the Laws of War regarding the treatment of prisoners, civilians, etc.

Which reminds me of a matter told of in Revelation 18:23:"for thy merchants were the great men of the earth; for by thy sorceries were all nations deceived" (especially our own nation and its people).

More than seventy years ago, I learned the Lord's Prayer; part of which went: "Thy kingdom come, Thy will be done, in (on) earth as it is in heaven." Can you imagine corporate enterprise, merchants, rich men, etc., a part of the heavenly scene? Can you imagine God approving of the actions of our country against the Vietnamese people; their schools; their hospitals; their crops; their children?

Well, I guess there was at least one religionist who must have thought so. Billy Graham was quite cozy with most of those five presidents who were part of the Vietnam episode.

In January 1968 a large group of Clergy and Laymen Concerned about Vietnam published a study that constituted an indictment of the United States conduct of the war. No, I don't see Billy Graham's name in that list of participants on page 521 of the Bertrand Russell Tribunal book.

I apologize for getting into my own thoughts on this matter. Now back to more of Master Sergeant Duncan's testimony to the tribunal.

Mr. Duncan had compared experiences in Vietnam with Robin Moore, author of *The Green Berets* and *A Country Team*, and another Green Beret, Peter Bourne. Their time in Vietnam spanned some three years and they all agreed that the torture of prisoners was consistent throughout—not a few isolated incidents. Duncan testified "More often than not—let me correct that—quite often the prisoners did not survive the interrogation."

About the civilian refugee camps (strategic hamlets, New Life hamlets):

> I have seen three or four of such camps. I used the word "garbage pit" for lack of a better euphemism, I suppose. The conditions under which these people are forced to live are, by any standards, appalling. There is usually a grave shortage of water, perhaps one water point for two hundred people. In other cases water has to be brought in, if there is any water at all. They are fortunate to have enough water for cooking and drinking, leaving very little over for sanitary purposes. The latrine facilities, if they exist at all, are of the worst order. There is very little for these people to do, no form of creative work. It's simply a matter of sitting around and letting time pass by. I didn't myself, see any evidence of physical abuse, in the sense of people going in there and just

systematically beating up refugees, but there was overcrowding, in the number of people living in one cubicle, for instance, in the provisions made for beds, which are usually nonexistent. You could usually smell these camps long before you came to them, because of the lack of sanitation facilities.—The Vietnamese are supposed to be the ones controlling these camps. More often than not it is the common thing that much of the money, food, clothing supplies, etc. never get to the people. It ends up in the black market or wherever. It's siphoned off. The provisions that they are supposed to get are minimal but then they only get a small percentage of that.

On the M-16 rifle:

The hitting effect of the M-16 is essentially a circumvention of the law prohibiting "dum dum" bullets. The bullet is very small in diameter—22 caliber—but it has a shell casing much larger—with the M-16 bullet, the bullet hits but does not have the tendency to penetrate, rather as it hits it tumbles. So in effect what we have now is a very big object trying to go through sideways. The effect of this, of course, is quite devastating.—To give you an idea of its hitting effect, on one combat operation at a relatively close range, I hit a man in the chest with one of these. It literally picked him up and hurled him back till he was stopped by a tree. He must have traveled about three or four feet off the ground and, of course, there was no chest left on the man. It was completely demolished. With a dum-dum bullet, which is an expanding bullet, though it would penetrate the body, it certainly would not have such a great effect. It's not only a circumvention, it's a magnification of the dum-dum effect.

Mr. Duncan, as stated earlier, was in Special Forces at the time of the Bay of Pigs invasion of Cuba, and relates how the Special Forces were in the Dominican Republic around that time, and:

Of course they are in Panama, in the Canal Zone, where we have our own School of the Americas, where we take people from these countries, such as Guatemala, Peru, Bolivia, Venezuela and so on, and we send them to that school for training by Special Forces. All of these things are very closely coordinated, of course, with CIA.—I think if you will make a study of it, that in every country in Latin America where we are involved and certainly in South Vietnam, it becomes readily apparent to even a casual visitor that these people are in grave need, long overdue need, for some type of social-political-economic revolution. Invariably they are being run by oligarchies, dictatorships or juntas of one sort or another. Instead of going into these countries and giving these people a revolution, by dealing directly with the people, the policy always is to go in and help the government—the rationale for this is, of course, that the government we're helping is anti-Communist. And so we are willing to overlook many of the imbalances, injustices, in many cases the corruption of these governments—in fact what we are doing is helping the very people that are responsible for the very conditions that exist and that made it necessary for you to get involved in the first place.

Supporting the above information related by Mr. Duncan, our Medford, Oregon, *Mail Tribune* for September 21, 1996, carried the following headline: U.S. ARMY TAUGHT TORTURE, EXECUTION.

The story that followed dealt with some instruction manuals used by the U.S. Army's School of the Americas founded in 1946 in Panama. (This was long before Fidel Castro and Che Guevera became prominent in Latin American affairs. Very likely there were already stirrings against the power elite factions of the region.)

The School was moved to Fort Benning, Georgia, in 1984, and finally in 1992 a Defense Department investigation uncovered the facts of what was taught to some sixty thousand military and police officers from eleven South and Central American countries over the years.

The findings of the investigation were finally released Friday night, September 20, 1996, *after* the deadlines of the prime time network television news programs.

In the manuals, neutralization was understood to mean the killing or destruction of personalities, installations, organizations, documents, and materials.

The manual says that to control things in the area, counter-intelligence agents could use fear, payment of bounties for enemy dead, beatings, false imprisonment, executions, and the use of truth serum. (I wonder how much bounty was paid for the capture and execution of Che Guevera.)

(As for false imprisonment, I believe Bolivia had a hostage crisis a year or so ago, where the hostage takers tried to bargain for the release of several hundred of their friends. Were these people some of the falsely imprisoned?)

Some of the graduates of the school included some of the region's most vicious human rights violators including Robert D'Aubuisson, the leader of El Salvador's right wing death squads; nineteen Salvadoran soldiers linked to the 1989 assassination of six Jesuit priests; and six Peruvian officers linked to killings of students, a professor, etc. General Manuel Antonio Noriega of Panama was also a graduate of the school.

The "problem" was discovered, reported, and fixed according to a Pentagon spokesman, Lieutenant Colonel Arne Owens.

(I wonder how many of those manuals have been recalled? How many of the graduates have been retrained to the new guidelines?)

There is a similar article in the Portland *Oregonian* for Mar. 6, 1997. Reporting that the manuals were ordered destroyed, the ostensible reason was so the materials could never be used again. "But Pentagon sources, who asked not to be named, said they suspect the documents were destroyed to hide an embarrassing chapter in the military's conduct abroad."

Instructions on how to torture, murder, etc., are merely embarrassing?

There was little follow-up on either of these articles, nothing like the Watergate investigations that forced the resignation of President Nixon; after he finally kept his promise to disengage us from Vietnam, seven years after his 1968 campaign promise; nothing like the on-going and never-ending investigation of the Whitewater (gate) scandal; and never-ending efforts to prove that the Clintons had lots to do with it. Could it be because Bill Clinton managed somehow to stay out of the Vietnam War, the pride and joy of the rich men who for so long have financed the political campaigns of so many of our leaders?

Mr. Duncan speaks of the infiltration of Special Forces/CIA missions into Laos and Cambodia—and North Vietnam. He says, "I was in Vietnam during the 1964 elections, when President Johnson was making certain statements relative to the war. He was in fact asking people to support the American official position in Vietnam, but I felt, in fact I had the visual proof, that he was not giving the facts to the American people on which they could make a reasonable decision. For instance, he was talking about getting ready to come home and getting out as soon as possible, and while he was making that same speech, the huge port facilities at Cam Ranh Bay were already well along in construction. He was talking about infiltration from North Vietnam and here in fact I was very closely involved with an operation where we were infiltrating North Vietnam, instead of North Vietnam infiltrating us. He talked about violations of the Geneva Agreements by the National Liberation Front and/or Hanoi???"

At one point Duncan gave his opinion that the United States Army never should have been in Vietnam in the first place. I wholeheartedly agree with his opinion on that.

V. The Roskilde Evidence—Part 2

Those three GIs, David Tuck, Peter Martinsen, and Donald Duncan, traveled all the way to Roskilde, Denmark, to testify before the Russell Tribunal. Several more GIs couldn't make the trip, but they sent tapes or depositions to the Tribunal of their observations.

Carl Campbell, speaking of his basic training in the Marines, declared, "They told us, that if we took prisoners and they became a burden to us, we should kill them."

> Question: "Do you know this is contrary to the Geneva Conventions?"
> Answer: "They didn't teach us in the Marines what those Conventions are. The people who taught us did not occupy themselves, I believe, with the Geneva Conventions."

Again on the subject of training and on the subject of ambushes, Campbell relates that an officer asked the trainees,

> "What would you do when you are on an operation if you see civilians or children in your line of fire?"
> No one answered. The officer then roared out: "Kill them!"

At Chu Lai, in the summer of 1965, his group left on an operation. Before entering the first village on their route, the officer said to them, verbatim: "You can kill anything with slanted eyes." The first Vietnamese they saw, an old man of about eighty years, was killed by a Marine. The Marine was immediately congratulated by the lieutenant and promoted two months later. The lieutenant slapped him on the shoulder and said, "That was a good shot, very well done." The officer added that the staff the old man was holding could have been a gun. Several months later this same soldier killed an old woman just as harmless.

Carl Campbell relates what happened to one of his "buddies" from another company, who had taken part in a difficult operation: "The Viet Cong had been cornered by the American forces with their backs to the sea. They had been furiously bombarded by air and artillery. When the bombardment ceased, my friend was one of those who went into the bombarded zone to see the effects. They found hundreds and hundreds of dead but all of them in civilian dress and only 40 rifles in the whole zone. The estimation of the number of dead varied between 600 and 1,000 civilians. And in other cases as well, those who are killed are called Viet Cong. Thus, they kill no civilians."

James Jones testified to facts directly under investigation by this Tribunal: 1) He saw two Vietnamese prisoners thrown from a U.S. helicopter; 2) He saw a woman burned by napalm, to whom medication was refused until she would talk; 3) He was present at the interrogation of a prisoner who had been bound and placed under the wheels of a truck. The truck was to start and crush him if he persisted in silence. Mr. Jones declares that though the tortures were the doing of Vietnamese functionaries, they were working under supervision of American officers who gave the instructions.

Jones added that the American troops had themselves: 1) burned villages; 2) executed a group of civilians; 3) destroyed an underground hospital in which all the patients perished.

James Clark Child, a bomber pilot, returned his war decorations to Secretary of Defense McNamara. His deposition included these statements:

"I served well as bombing pilot for nearly 18 months in Vietnam (1966–1967). I completed 17 bombing missions. Twelve of these missions were deliberately directed against civilian targets. I myself dropped high explosive and incendiary bombs against farms, villages and forests.

I became aware that I was killing women and children, and I went to protest to my officer, indicating that I would refuse any future missions of that kind. He answered that it was necessary to obey orders from Washington. Soon after my gesture of protest, I was sent home.

In my letter to McNamara, I declared verbatim: "My friends and the Vietnamese are dying every day for the ideologies held by leaders who do not understand the proportions of this foolish and agonizing war in Vietnam. I cannot in my soul and conscience, uphold the policy of escalation and of massive incessant bombardment of North Vietnam."

A Dr. Erich Wulff, a member of a West German Medical Mission to Vietnam, tells a lengthy story of his observations:

Ladies and Gentlemen—I have just arrived from South Vietnam and I have had no time to draft a text. I decided to come here before this Tribunal for two main reasons: One, because in the six years I spent in Vietnam, I saw a certain number of things which revolted me; and when the opportunity occurred to come here, I seized it immediately. Secondly, because a number of my Vietnamese friends who are rendered silent at the present time, asked me to come here and speak in their stead.—Everyone who flies over South Vietnam now can see that the landscape resembles a human skin that suffers from smallpox. There are eruptions everywhere caused by bomb craters which are especially close to isolated habitations, little hamlets, little valleys. Everyone who flies over the land can see it and can draw his own conclusions. In flying over the country, also you can see vast areas which are destroyed and devastated by chemical products. It is a grave landscape—a landscape of ashes. You see, especially in the coastal region, in the province of Quang Nam, close by Phou Yon, chains of villages, habitations, and rice fields, that have been abandoned—a blanket of death—a landscape of death. One need not be an expert to draw conclusions.

When one goes a little more deeply into events and into the techniques used by the Americans, one can distinguish several main ways by which the war is conducted. The most standard technique is "search and destroy" operations. What happens is that a number of helicopters will land in a village. The soldiers enter the houses, they take a certain number of people who live there, especially young ones and women. They arrest them on the pretext that they are suspected "Vietcong" and they take them to interrogation centers. The rest of the population has endured this ceaselessly. It is a nightmare of the Thirty Years War. After a time the helicopters fly off, and the population remains, stricken with terror and fear. Now what happens to these prisoners? I have the occasion while working at the Central Hospital of Hue to see about fifty prisoners from the neighboring prisons who were sent to the hospital in extremely serious conditions, sometimes just before they died. Two examples follow.

Mr. "X," a farmer of thirty years, was living in Pen Dim, in the province of Quang Dien. He has been an orphan since childhood. He is married with two children. Condition: poor. He had been in prison three years before being sent to the hospital with a condition of beriberi. The man had been arrested in a raiding operation without any evidence of his guilt. He was suspected of being a Vietcong. He was tortured by kicks on his chest, head, his belly, and then by electric wires wound around the forefinger. After this, he preferred to sign the confession that was presented to him already written. Penalty: four years of prison. After this he was evacuated to the prison of Hue, where he was imprisoned.

The second example, a young girl of 20, living in Top Ku, in the province of Tun Tang, a farmer's daughter, unmarried, living with her parents in a large family. She had been in prison for two years. The arrest was quite identical with the first case—she had been arrested in the course of a raiding operation as a Vietcong suspect. She was tortured, beaten with sticks and given the electric torture. She was made to drink soapy water. The result was that she signed an avowal and was convicted to two years in prison. These are typical cases, and I shall submit them to the Tribunal. There are a few others; there are also, of course, some men and woman who did not confess and their stories are much worse. They are tortured for a much longer time. No judgment by a court is usually pronounced, and they remain in prison or in a prisoner's camp for an indefinite time. Most of them were simple peasants who lived quietly at home, and whose only wrong was of not having fled in time.

Dr. Wulff went into some detail on how the American policy removed the entire population from a given area, a large area, and had generated some 2 million refugees and put in camps variously called "strategic hamlets" and "new life hamlets" near military camps.

He also remarked on civilians burned by napalm treated by him, and also treated on the West German hospital ship the *Helgoland*. He also treated burns from toxic concentrations of supposed tear gas. On tortures: "The Americans, with their hygienic spirit, have an obsession with not getting their hands dirty. So they use the South Vietnamese police and the South Vietnamese so-called elite troops to carry out the tortures—in 80 percent of the cases, the tortures are executed by the South Vietnamese troops while the Americans remain to the side—this was, for me, one of the most disgusting aspects of American behavior in Vietnam, as was their blind bombing of villages."

Jean Bertolino, a French journalist, told of several incidents while accompanying the American forces. Of the several operations he was on, the last:

At the Market-Place of Rach Kien, I searched the miserable mass of people which has lived abandoned in degrading poverty in the midst of the enormous American war-machine looking for youths of 15, of 20, or men of 30. The only adolescents I ever saw were held on a leash.

Several hours earlier in the trenches, some 100 meters from the village, these boys had been lying in wait with gun in hand for the comings and goings of the GIs. Perhaps it was one of them who, on the day of my arrival, had fired a bullet full in the face of two young US recruits. They had not listened to the warnings of the colonel, who had enjoined them not to leave the security perimeter.

A punitive expedition was organized. Half of the brigade and a unit of General Ky's Special Forces left to sweep the countryside. The four Vietcong, not even 20 years old, were surprised by young Vietnamese who could have been their brothers. They were led to the center of Rach Kien. No trial, no sentence. It was 7:00 o'clock—the American soldiers retired into their perimeter. The South Vietnamese mercenaries, one of whom had tattooed on his chest, "I kill Vietcong and I love my country," ordered the prisoners to kneel, the population was energetically encouraged to come and witness the spectacle. The young militiamen pulled machetes from their belts and with a sharp slash they decapitated the four Vietcong. Seeing my cameras, they held the bloody heads by the hair, placed cigarettes in their mouths, and cried to me, "Come on take photo, take photo." I have, as you know, submitted these photos to the Tribunal as evidence.

On the subject of the Koreans to whom Sergeant Duncan just alluded in his deposition, I wish to testify that their primary mission is to assure the proper functioning of the pipeline which connects Pleiku to Qui Nonh. It seems that they fulfilled this mission perfectly, for the simple reason that each time that there were incidents along the pipeline, the South Koreans went into the nearest village to massacre the population indiscriminately at one fell swoop.

Mr. Bertolino went into some detail on the corruption and prostitution in and around Saigon and the military bases.

Madelain Riffaud, a French journalist and author of several books about conditions in Vietnam, testified before the Tribunal. She carried out investigations in Vietnam from January to May 1955, from the end of November 1964 to the beginning of February 1965 and also north of the 17th Parallel in the summer and autumn of 1966.

In the first days of the Diem regime, the people were divided into categories: Category A, "those suspected of being former resistance fighters," and Category B, "families of former resistance fighters." Arrests, torturing before the assembled village population, humiliations, executions pure and simple—all these began to be employed against people in these categories. "Repentance meetings" were organized by Diem agents, advised by psychological warfare experts sent from Washington. These were aimed at forcing the people to deny publicly their patriotic convictions.

Wives of former resistance fighters were subjected to a "divorce campaign." They were given prepared forms by the police, who forced them to sign a declaration according to which they disowned their husbands or fiancées or sons in the North. The unhappy women refused. Their children were taken from them, under the pretext of raising them as "anti-Communists." One woman herself was taken away and tortured in one of the many military security areas which had been set up by the thousands for the occasion in schools, pagodas, unused churches. In a short time all of South Vietnam came to resemble an immense concentration camp. The tortures to obtain divorces and disavowals include: the soles of the feet were beaten, fingertips were pierced, preferred were those tortures which brought about sterility. One which was practiced was "exorcism," in which the victim was tied in a sack, pierced with swords, doused with gasoline and burned to the accompaniments of drums.

I learned quite by chance that in October 1959, a law set forth in Saigon provided that it was enough to have been found guilty by the special military courts of subversive "intentions" against the government to be condemned to life imprisonment or death; without preliminary investigation, without any confession from the accused. Sentences against which there was no appeal were carried out at once. Entire families were wiped out during this period, and portable guillotines went from village to village.

All of this under the "I like IKE," administration, with John Foster Dulles as Secretary of State, and Allen Dulles as head of the CIA. The Dulles brothers were co-conspirators with Hitler's Third Reich; in setting up the "America First" movement, they intended to prevent America's entry into the European conflict.

In the villages of An Tanh, An Hoa, An Ninh, and Duc Hoa, four schools were burned and destroyed in one month of October 1964. At An Hoa, where I spent a sleepless night with the inhabitants. I saw the napalm-blackened ruins of the school, the bamboo trunks which had held up the roof stark against the sky. And the people showed me the pitiful remains; blood-spattered arithmetic books, caps with bullet holes in them, little articles of half-burned clothing that had belonged to the murdered children or to those being cared for in the hospital. I am unable to go into all the statements and evidence I collected; I shall confine myself to events in An Hoa. But the others are equally heartbreaking. Here is an example of such a testimony:

It was at a time when all the children were in school. The evening before, propaganda helicopters had passed over and dropped leaflets and had threatened the people by loud speaker with reprisals if they continued to refuse to move to strategic hamlets. They were the HU-1A which are able to hang in the air and are used as firing platforms. The next day they returned. As you saw, we built the school on open ground. We put a sign on the facade: *Communal School.* We were still too trusting, despite all the wrongs which had been done us. We thought that when they saw the sign the airplanes would not make a mistake and bomb the school—they didn't make a mistake. Right at the beginning, their reconnaissance plane dropped smoke bombs in the school courtyard to point out the target.

There were two classes in the school. The top form, led by its teacher, got to the shelters safely in a disciplined manner. In the kindergarten classes, sixty children from 5 to 7 years of age became frightened and grabbed hold of their teacher who was trying to calm them, or hid beneath their desks and refused to come out. The teacher, who was 20 years old, knew from experience that the helicopters would fire rockets into the classroom. Unable to get the children out in time for them to take refuge in the trenches, he tried to get them into the corners of the room. But the rocket fire had already begun. The first explosions occurred by the exit, which turned into a wall of fire.

The teacher then tried to get the children out the window by threes, carrying one on his back and one under each arm. In this way, he made more than ten trips under heavy rocket and machine gun fire. However, many children were killed or injured in the classroom itself and everyone was in a state of panic.

Tam, the teacher, succeeded in evacuating 45 children before he was hit. Injured in the leg, he made one more trip, but on his return he was hit again, this time badly. Thinking that he was dying, he shouted to the children in the building who were still alive, "Get out through the window, don't be afraid; I'm hurt but I'm still here."

"Big brother," the children called back, "we can't get out through the window; we're too little—" (I know this is exact, since it was told to me by Tam, the teacher, who survived.)

At that instant, the planes dropped napalm on what was left of the school. And not another sound was heard from the children.

On the outside, the children which Tam had evacuated with such difficulty had come out of the dugouts because they were afraid, and tried to run to their homes. On the road, they were machine-gunned by low flying helicopters which hunted them down like rabbits. They flew so low that the American uniforms could be clearly made out.

There are several reports on the torture of woman prisoners. One of them is the testimony of Mrs. Pham Thi Yen:

On April 18, 1960 at 8:00 P.M., right in the streets of Saigon, the US-Diemist security police arrested me because of my patriotic activities. I was taken to the Commando Post Number 1, the Ba Hoa Post at Cho Lon. The commandant himself directed the interrogation, which started immediately after my arrest. He put questions about my activities with the patriots. I did not reply to these questions, so they started to torture me. Reeking with alcohol, the "commandos" as the Vietnamese call them, started beating me, shouting with rage. The commandos are a sort of Vietnamese Gestapo.

They tied my arms behind my back, then hauled me up to the ceiling by strong cords attached to my wrists. They beat me with sticks, stopping only when I fainted. Then they let me down, throwing cold water over my face. Little by little I recovered consciousness. More questions. Silence. Furious, they hung me up again. This was repeated I don't know how many times. They called this operation "ride in a Dakota."

My body was covered with wounds and was most painfully swollen. I suffered atrociously—the slightest movement and I thought I would faint with pain.

After a moment's rest, they applied the "ride in a submarine." They undressed me and tied me, face upward, to a plank. A towel was used to tie my head to the plank; a rubber tube led from a 200-liter barrel, fixed to a stand. The water fell drop by drop onto the towel, soon flooding my face. To breathe I sucked in water through my nose and mouth. I was suffocating, my stomach started to swell like a balloon. I could no longer breathe and I fainted. When I regained consciousness, I suffered unimaginable pains. I opened my eyes and saw two commandos called Duc and Danh, and nicknamed the "Gray Tigers" because of their blood-curdling, exploits, stamping on my chest and stomach to get the water out of me. I vomited through my mouth and nose, water mixed with blood pouring out. This was repeated several times. I suffered atrociously in my chest and in my stomach; it was as if someone was twisting my entrails.

"Serve her another dish," the commander said to his agents. The latter formed a square and with myself in the center, they beat me with sticks. They pushed me from one to another as if I were a Ping-Pong ball, shouting and hurling insults at me. I was seriously wounded in the head, blood trickled down. They stopped beating me and started to shave my head, to bandage it.

They started to lull me with doubtful promises mixed with threats—

"Talk, and you can rejoin your children. If not, you will die and your children will be orphans."

"Talk, or we will torture you to death and even if you survive you'll be useless, without strength to brush a fly away."

Neither their sickening promises nor their threats had any effect. Screaming with rage, they threw my face down on the floor, a huge brute squatting on my back, two others holding my feet with the soles turned upwards. Using police truncheons they beat the soles of my feet with all their strength. My feet and legs swelled up visibly as they struck. I felt as if my skin was going to burst.

Afterward they hung me by my wrists, this time attached to the iron bars of a window with handcuffs, my arms crossed at a height at which I could only stand on the tips of my toes. My arms and legs hurt terribly. They started to hammer my arms against the bars. My arms became numb. Seeing this had no effect, they untied me and kicked me on to the floor again. They started to kick me. Blood was running all over the place. I fainted.

Again there were promises, threats and insults. Tired themselves, they called other prisoners and tried to force them to beat me. They all refused, so the prisoners were furiously beaten. In that place there was no room for human sentiments at all.

Just before dawn they said they would serve me a "sensational dish." They attached me to a kaki tree in the garden near a cage where two tigers were ferociously roaring. In South Vietnam, kaki trees, which produce very sweet fruit, are always covered with yellow ants. If a single ant stings you, you'll yell with pain. And the spot where you are stung will swell up immediately with the effect of the poison. This tree was just of this species–its branches full of yellow ants...

The tigers continued roaring, the torturers were shouting with rage. It was a frightful and at the same time terribly sinister experience. But all this also had no effect. My feelings were entirely concentrated on the little ants, and their stings were so painful.

The torturers threatened me: "If you don't talk, your children will be tortured in front of your eyes; your parents, your brothers and sisters will be imprisoned. Your family will be destroyed; your pharmacy seized..."

At 6 o'clock in the morning, after ten hours of torture, they threw me into a cell. I could hardly stand up. I had to lie down on the cold floor....

In the foregoing testimony of Mrs. Pham Thi Yen about the two torturers nicknamed the "Gray Tigers," it struck me that another Vietnamese, Lt. Col. Phong, nicknamed "Tiger" by his American advisor, Lt. Col. Earl Woods, might well have earned that nickname for reasons similar. There is a lengthy story on the search for "Tiger" Phong in the October and November 1997 *Golf Digest*, the search for "Tiger" Woods's nicknamesake.

"Tiger" Phong visited his family before giving himself up to the Communist government that took over South Vietnam as American forces finally finished vacating the country. If he died in a re-education camp of starvation, as suggested by the story by Tom Callahan, there surely were a lot of Vietnamese who must have died of starvation also, as a result of the vast destruction of crops and cropland by American forces with "Agent Orange" and other defoliants.

There is one thing that became obvious in the story. Compared to the treatment of Viet Minh forces and their families under the Diem regime, and under the direction of American advisors in the late 1950s and early 1960s (hunted down, arrested, imprisoned, tortured, executed, etc.)—the "Tiger" Phong family was apparently never harassed, or mistreated by the Communist forces. Some are here in America, including "Tiger" Phong's widow and three children. The rest are still alive and well in South Vietnam.

As for the nickname "Tiger," I wonder, in relation to Lt. Col. Phong's actions in the war, what did he do that earned him that nickname by his American advisor? And what did his American advisor teach him about American wishes in the treatment of his fellow countrymen? "Tiger" Woods has become a multimillionaire before his twenty-first birthday, thanks to his father's guidance and "advice," and his product endorsements. He has *earned* another $2 million plus in his twenty-first year of life on the PGA tour. What "Tiger" Phong did to his people is no reflection on our beginning golf pro.

It is likewise no bad reflection on either "Tiger" Phong or Earl Woods, because they were following orders from Washington. And the politicians were only doing the wishes of their campaign contributors, the wealth interests of our nation. And for the same reason, the European governments never seriously challenged our Vietnam actions because their governments are likewise controlled by the wealthy interests of their nations—the same interests that approved of what Hitler did to the 6 million Jews, and to 28 million of the Soviet Union forces and civilians, including many Jews.

It is a good sign that attention is being paid to campaign financing, but I seriously doubt if the investigation will go far enough or dig deeply enough, to correct the whole situation.

It is interesting how often something appears in the news about that period of time. Not long ago some Johnson tapes were released and disclosed that Johnson had felt that Castro had had something to do with the JFK assassination—but he wouldn't press the issue for fear that 40 million Americans would die in the first hour if a nuclear war should ensue over Cuba.

Again, not long ago, a bunch of Montagnards claimed that they had not yet been paid for a lot of the time they had served under Special Forces in Vietnam.

And again, just recently a large bunch of Vietnamese Special Forces, who had been infiltrated into North Vietnam (while the US government was claiming North Vietnam was infiltrating the South, according to Donald Duncan), were captured almost immediately, and spent some twenty years imprisoned there. Now they want back pay for all that time in captivity.

And just a few days ago, there was news of an effort to find out the fate of some 400 to 500 MIAs (missing in action) in Laos. Donald Duncan briefly mentioned his part in planning Special Forces forays into Laos and Cambodia. But that many MIAs where it was supposed to be a neutral nation?

Wilfred Burchett explains the history of American intervention into Laos, from 1954 when one Laotian delegate refused to sign the Geneva Agreements, and a million dollars was put into a Swiss bank account in his name as a reward. The other, who did sign the agreement for Laos, was assassinated just two months later while an invited guest for dinner at the first delegate's invitation. From then on it was a continuous and ongoing effort on the part of America to control Laos as well as Vietnam. There must have been enormous American troop involvement for that many MIAs to be unaccounted for. Mr. Burchett outlines the involvement in a little over four pages.

There are several chapters detailing the complicity and involvement of Thailand, Japan, and the Philippines in support of America in the Vietnam War.

Jean Paul Sartre, Executive President of the Tribunal, and Lelio Basso, International Lawyer and Deputy of Italian Parliament, sum up the issue of Genocide by the American forces against the Vietnamese, Laotians, and Cambodians in some thirty pages; by Sartre:

> There have been cases, however, in which the genocidal response to people's war is not checked by the infrastructure contradictions. Then total genocide emerges as the absolute basis of an anti-guerrilla strategy. And under certain conditions it even emerges

as the explicit objective—sought either immediately or by degrees. This is precisely what is happening in the Vietnam War. We are dealing here with a new stage in the development of imperialism, a stage usually called neo-colonialism because it is characterized by aggression against a former colony which has already gained its independence, with the aim of subjugating it anew to colonial rule. With the beginning of independence, the neo-colonialists take care to finance a putsch or coup d'etat so that the new heads of state do not represent the interests of the masses but rather those of a narrow privileged strata, and, consequently, of foreign capital.

Ngo Dinh Diem appeared—hand-picked, maintained and armed by the United States. He proclaimed his decision to reject the Geneva Agreements and to constitute the Vietnamese territory to the south of the 17th parallel as an independent state. What followed was the necessary consequence of these premises; a police force and an army were created to hunt down people who had fought against the French, and who now felt thwarted of their victory, a sentiment which automatically marked them as enemies of the new regime. In short, it was the reign of terror which provoked a new uprising in the south and rekindled the people's war.

Did the United States ever imagine that Diem could nip the revolt in the bud? In any event, they lost no time in sending in experts and then troops, and then they were involved in the conflict up to their necks. And we find once again almost the same pattern of war as the one that Ho Chi Minh fought against the French, except that at first the American government declared that it was only sending in troops out of generosity, to fulfill its obligations to an ally.

That is the outward appearance. But looking deeper, these two successive wars are essentially different in character; the United States, unlike France, has no economic interests in Vietnam. American firms have some investments, but not so much that they couldn't be sacrificed, if necessary, without troubling the American nation as a whole or really hurting the monopolies.

Moreover, since the U.S. government is not waging the war for reasons of a directly economic nature, there is nothing to stop it from ending the war by the ultimate tactic—in other words, by genocide. This is not to say that there is proof that the U.S. does in fact envision genocide, but simply that nothing prevents the U.S. from envisaging it.

In fact, according to the Americans themselves, the conflict has two objectives. Just recently, Dean Rusk stated: "We are defending ourselves." It is no longer Diem the ally whom the Americans are generously helping out; it is the United States itself which is in danger in Saigon. Obviously, this means that the first objective is a military one; to encircle Communist China. Therefore, the United States will not let Southeast Asia escape. It has put its men in power in Thailand, it controls two-thirds of Laos and threatens to invade Cambodia. But these conquests will be hollow if it finds itself confronted by a free and unified Vietnam with 32 million inhabitants. That is why the military leaders like to talk in terms of "key positions." That is why Dean Rusk says, with unintentional humor, that the armed forces of the United States are fighting in Vietnam "in order to win this third conflict." In short the first objective is dictated by the necessity of establishing a Pacific line of defense, something which is necessary only in the context of the general policy of imperialism.

The second objective is an economic one. In October 1966, General Westmoreland defined it as follows: "We are fighting the war in Vietnam to show that guerrilla warfare does not pay." To show whom? The Vietnamese? That would be very surprising. Must so many human lives and so much money be wasted merely to teach a lesson to a nation of poor peasants thousands of miles from San Francisco? And in particular, what need was there to attack them, provoke them into fighting and subsequently to go about crushing them, when the big American companies have only negligible interests in Vietnam? Westmoreland's statement, like Rusk's, has to be filled in. The Americans want to show others that guerrilla war does not pay; they want to show all the oppressed and exploited nations that might be tempted to shake off the American yoke by launching a people's war, at first against their own pseudo-governments, the compradors and the army, then against the US "Special Forces," and finally against the GIs. In short, they want to show Latin America first of all, and more generally, all of the Third World. To Che Guevara who said, "We need several more Vietnams," the American government answers, "They will all be crushed the way we are crushing the first."

In other words, this war has above all an admonitory value, as an example for three and perhaps four continents. This genocidal example is addressed to the whole of humanity. By means of this warning, 6 percent of mankind hopes to succeed in controlling the other 94 percent at a reasonable low cost in money and effort.

The declarations of American statesmen are not as candid as Hitler's were in his day. But candor is not essential to us here. It is enough that the facts speak; the speeches which come with them are believed only by the American people. The rest of the world understands well enough; governments which are friends of the United States keep silent; the others denounce this genocide. The Americans try to reply that these unproved accusations only show these governments' partiality. "In fact," the American government says, "all we have ever done is to offer the Vietnamese, North and South, the option of ceasing their aggression or being crushed." It is scarcely necessary to mention that this offer is absurd, since it is the Americans who commit the aggression and consequently they are the only ones who can put an end to it. But this absurdity is not undeliberate; the Americans are ingeniously formulating, without appearing to do so, a demand which the Vietnamese cannot satisfy. They do offer an alternative: Declare you are beaten or we will bomb you back to the stone age. But the fact remains that the second term of this alternative is genocide. They have said: "Genocide, yes, but conditional genocide." Is this juridically valid? Is it even conceivable?

If the proposition made any juridical sense at all, the US government might narrowly escape the accusation of genocide. But the 1948 Convention leaves no such loopholes; an act of genocide, especially if it is carried out over a period of several years, is no less genocide for being blackmail. The perpetrator may declare he will stop if the victim gives in; this is still—without any juridical doubt whatsoever—a genocide. And this is all the more true when, as is the case here, a good part of the group has been annihilated to force the rest to give in.

But let us look at this more closely and examine the nature of the two terms of the alternative. In the south, the choice is the following: villages burned, the populace subjected to massive bombing, livestock shot, vegetation destroyed by defoliants, crops ruined by toxic aerosols, and everywhere indiscriminate shooting, murder, rape and looting. This is genocide in the strictest sense; massive extermination. The other option; what is it? What are the Vietnamese people supposed to do to escape this horrible death? Join the armed forces of Saigon or be enclosed in strategic or today's "New Life" hamlets, two names for the same concentration camps?

We know about these camps from numerous witnesses. They are fenced in by barbed wire. Even the most elementary needs are denied; there is malnutrition and total lack of hygiene. The prisoners are heaped together in small tents or sheds. The social structure is destroyed. Husbands are separated from their wives, mothers from their children; family life, so important to the Vietnamese, no longer exists. As families are split up, the birth rate falls; any possibility of religious or cultural life is suppressed; even work—the work which might permit people to maintain themselves and even their families—is refused them. These unfortunate people are not even slaves (slavery did not prevent the Negroes in the United States from developing a rich culture); they are reduced to a living heap of vegetable existence. When, sometimes, a fragmented family group is freed—children with an elder sister or a young mother—it goes to swell the ranks of the sub-proletariat in the big cities; the elder sister or the mother, with no job and mouths to feed, reaches the last stage of degradation in prostituting herself to the GIs.

The camps I described are but another kind of genocide, equally condemned by the 1948 Convention:

"Causing serious bodily or mental harm to members of the group."

"Deliberately inflicting on the group conditions of life calculated to bring about its physical destruction in whole or in part."

"Imposing measures intended to prevent births within the group."

"Forcibly transferring children of the group to another group."

In other words, it is not true the choice is between death or submission. For submission, in those circumstances, is submission to genocide. Let us say that a choice must be made between a violent and immediate death and a slow death from mental and physical degradation. Or, if you prefer, there is no choice at all.

Is it any different for the North?

One choice is extermination. Not just the daily risk of death, but the systematic destruction of the economic base of the country; from the dikes to the factories, nothing will be left standing. Deliberate attacks against civilians, and, in particular, the rural population. Systematic destruction of hospitals, schools and places of worship. An all out campaign to destroy the achievements of 20 years of socialism. The purpose may be only to intimidate the populace. But this can only be achieved by the daily extermination of an ever larger part of the group. So this intimidation itself in its psycho-social consequences is a genocide. Among the children in particular it must be engendering psychological disorders which will for years, if not permanently, "cause serious—mental harm."

The other choice is capitulation. This means that the North Vietnamese must declare themselves ready to stand by and watch while their country is divided and the Americans impose a direct or indirect dictatorship on their compatriots, in fact on members of their own families from whom the war has separated them. And would this intolerable humiliation bring an end to the war? This is far from certain. The National Liberation Front and the Democratic Republic of Vietnam, although fraternally united, have different strategies and tactics because their war situations are different. If the NLF continued the struggle, American bombs would go on blasting the DRV whether it capitulated or not.

If the war were to cease, the United States—according to official statements—would feel generously inclined to help in the reconstruction of the DRV, and we know exactly what this means. It means that the United States would destroy, through private investments and conditional loans, the whole economic base of socialism. And this too is genocide. They would be splitting a sovereign country in half, occupying one of the halves by a reign of terror and keeping the other half under control by economic pressure. The "national group" Vietnam would not be physically eliminated, yet it would no longer exist. Economically, politically and culturally it would be suppressed.

In the North as in the South, the choice is only between two types of liquidation: collective death or dismemberment. The American government has ample opportunity to test the resistance of the NLF and the DRV; by now it knows that only total destruction will be effective. The Front is stronger than ever; North Vietnam is unshakable. For this very reason, the calculated extermination of the Vietnamese people cannot really be intended to make them capitulate. The Americans offer then a *paix des braves*, knowing full well that they will not accept it. And this phony alternative hides the true goal of imperialism, which is to reach, step by step, the highest stage of escalation—total genocide.

Meanwhile, the major purpose of "escalation" was, and still is, to prepare international opinion for genocide. From this point of view, Americans have succeeded only too well. The repeated and systematic bombings of populated areas of Haiphong and Hanoi, which two years ago would have raised violent protests in Europe, occur today in a climate of general indifference resulting perhaps more from catatonia than from apathy. The tactic has borne its fruit; public opinion now sees escalation as a slowly and continuously increasing pressure to bargain, while in reality it is the preparation of minds for the final genocide. Is such a genocide possible? No. But that is due to the Vietnamese and the Vietnamese alone; to their courage, and to the remarkable efficiency of their organization. As for the United States government, it cannot be absolved of its crime just because its victim has enough intelligence and enough heroism to limit its effects.

We may conclude that in the face of a people's war (the characteristic product of our times, the answer to imperialism and the demand for sovereignty of a people conscious of its unity) there are two possible responses; either the aggressor withdraws, he acknowledges that a whole nation confronts him, and he makes peace, or else he recognizes the inefficacy of conventional strategy, and, if he can do so without jeopardizing his interests, he resorts to extermination pure and simple. There is no third alternative, but making peace is still at least possible.

But as the armed forces of the USA entrench themselves firmly in Vietnam, as they intensify the bombing and the massacres, as they try to bring Laos under their control, as they plan the invasion of Cambodia, there is less and less doubt that the government of the United States, despite its hypocritical denials, has chosen genocide.

The genocidal intent is implicit in the facts. It is necessarily premeditated. Perhaps in bygone times, in the midst of tribal wars, acts of genocide were perpetrated on the spur of the moment in fits of passion. But the anti-guerrilla genocide which our times have produced requires organization, military bases, a structure of accomplices, budget appropriations. Therefore, its authors must meditate and plan out their act. Does this mean that they are thoroughly conscious of their intentions? It is impossible to decide. We would have to plumb the depths of their consciences—and the Puritan bad faith of Americans works wonders.

There are probably people in the State Department who have become so used to fooling themselves that they still think they are working for the good of the Vietnamese people. However, we may only surmise that there are fewer and fewer of these hypocritical innocents after the recent statements of their spokesmen: "We are defending ourselves; even if the Saigon government begged us, we would not leave Vietnam, etc. etc." At any rate, we don't have to concern ourselves with this psychological hide-and-seek. The truth is apparent on the battlefield in the racism of the American soldiers.

This racism—anti-black, anti-Asiatic, anti-Mexican—is a basic American attitude with deep historical roots and which existed, latently and overtly, well before the Vietnamese conflict. One proof of this is that the United States government refused to ratify the Geneva Convention. This doesn't mean that in 1948 the US intended to exterminate a people; what it does mean—according to the statements of the US Senate—is that the Convention would conflict with the laws of several states; in other words, the current policy makers enjoy a free hand in Vietnam because their predecessors catered to the anti-black racism of Southern whites. In any case, since 1966, the racism of Yankee soldiers, from Saigon to the 17th parallel, has become more and more marked. Young American men use torture (even including the "field telephone" treatment—the portable generator of a field telephone is used as an instrument for torture by attaching the lead wires to the victim's genitals and turning the handle. The apparatus delivers a severe painful shock), they shoot unarmed women for nothing more than target practice, they kick wounded Vietnamese in the genitals, they cut off ears of dead men to take home for trophies. Officers are the worst; a general boasted of hunting "VCs" from his helicopter and gunning them down in the rice paddies. Obviously, these were not NLF soldiers who knew how to defend themselves; they were peasants tending their rice. In the confused minds of the American soldiers, "Viet Cong" and "Vietnamese" tend increasingly to blend into one another. They often say themselves, "The only good Vietnamese is a dead Vietnamese," or what amounts to the same thing, "A dead Vietnamese is a Viet Cong."

For example, south of the 17th parallel, peasants prepare to harvest their rice. American soldiers arrive on the scene, set fire to their houses and want to transfer them to a strategic hamlet. The peasants protest. What else can they do, barehanded against these Martians? They say: "The quality of the rice is good; we want to stay and eat our rice.'' Nothing more. But this is enough to irritate the young Yankees; "It's the Viet Cong who put that into your head; they are the ones who have taught you to resist." These soldiers are so misled that they take the feeble protests which their own violence has aroused for "subversive" resistance. At the outset, they were probably disappointed; they came to save Vietnam from "communist aggressors." But they soon had to realize that the Vietnamese did not want them. Their attractive role as liberators changed to that of occupation troops. For the soldiers it was the first glimmering of consciousness; "We are unwanted, we have no business here." But they go no further. They simply tell themselves that a Vietnamese is by definition suspect.

And from the neo-colonialists' point of view, this is true. They vaguely understand that in a people's war, civilians are the only visible enemies. Their frustration turns to hatred of the Vietnamese; racism takes it from there. The soldiers discover with a savage joy that they are there to kill the Vietnamese they had been pretending to save. All of them are potential Communists, as proved by the fact that they hate Americans.

Now we can recognize in those dark and misled souls the truth of the Vietnam war; it meets all of Hitler's specifications. Hitler killed the Jews because they were Jews. The armed forces of the United States torture and kill men, women and children in Vietnam merely because they are Vietnamese. Whatever lies or euphemisms the government may think up, the spirit of genocide is in the minds of the soldiers. This is their way of living out the genocidal situation into which their government has thrown them. As Peter Martinsen, a 23-year-old student who had "interrogated" prisoners for ten months and could scarcely live with his memories, said: "I am a middle class American. I look like any other student, yet somehow I am a war criminal." And he was right when he added: "Anyone in my place would have acted as I did." His only mistake was to attribute his degrading crimes to the influence of war in general.

No, it is not war in the abstract; it is the greatest power on the earth against a poor peasant people. Those who fight it are living out the only possible relationship between an over-industrialized country and an underdeveloped country, that is to say, a genocidal relationship implemented through racism—the only relationship, short of picking up and pulling out.

Total war presupposes a certain balance of forces, a certain reciprocity. Colonial wars were not reciprocal, but the interests of the colonialists limited the scope of genocide. The present genocide, the end result of the unequal development of societies, is total war waged to the limit by one side, without the slightest reciprocity.

The American government is not guilty of inventing modern genocide, or even of having chosen it from other possible and effective measures against guerrilla warfare. It is not guilty, for example, of having preferred genocide for strategic and economic reasons. Indeed, genocide presents itself as the only possible reaction to the rising of a whole people against its oppressors.

The American government is guilty of having preferred, and of still preferring, a policy of war and aggression aimed at total genocide to a policy of peace, the only policy which can really replace the former. A policy of peace would necessarily have required a reconsideration of the objectives imposed on that government by the large imperialist companies through the intermediary of their pressure groups. America is guilty of continuing and intensifying the war despite the fact that every day its leaders realize more acutely, from the reports of the military commanders, that the only way to win is "to free Vietnam of all the Vietnamese." The government is guilty—despite the lessons it has been taught by this unique, unbearable experience—of proceeding at every moment a little further along a path which leads it to the point of no return. And it is guilty—according to its own admissions—of consciously carrying out this admonitory war in order to use genocide as a challenge and a threat to all peoples of the world.

We have seen that one of the features of total war has been the growing scope of efficiency of communication. As early as 1914, war could no longer be "localized." It had to spread throughout the whole world. In 1967, this process is being intensified. The ties of the "One World," on which the United States wants to impose its hegemony, have grown tighter and tighter. For this reason, as the American government very well knows, the current genocide is conceived as an answer to people's war and perpetrated in Vietnam not against the Vietnamese alone, but against humanity.

When a peasant falls in his rice paddy, mowed down by a machine gun, every one of us is hit. The Vietnamese fight for all men and the American forces [fight] against all. Neither figuratively nor abstractly. And not only because genocide would be a crime universally condemned by international law, but because little by little the whole human race is being subjected to this genocidal blackmail piled on top of atomic blackmail, that is, to absolute, total war. This crime, carried out every day before the eyes of the world, renders all who do not denounce it accomplices of those who commit it, so that we are being degraded today for our future enslavement.

In this sense imperialist genocide can only become more complete. The group which the United States wants to intimidate and terrorize by way of the Vietnamese nation is the human group in its entirety.

So much for Jean Paul Sartre's reasoned and cogent comments on the genocidal aspects of America's aggressive war against the nation and peoples of Vietnam.

Lelio Basso reviews a lot of the reports and evidence previously covered, and then in part two of his dissertation covers comments made by leaders over the years, since the War of 1812, on the needs for expansionism, which include spreading west to the Pacific shores, then to Hawaii, Cuba, and the Philippines. He speaks of the role of America since World War II, and remarks on the new policy of "Globalism."

"The doctrine of 'globalism' is a doctrine to justify American intervention in every part of the world. It is the theory held by a whole school of foreign policy makers. The result has been that it is not the now petrified apparatus of the United Nations, but the unilateral decision of the US that decides, if, where and how the US should intervene without concern for the will of the interested parties."

Walt Whitman Rostow has defined the aim, which is to establish everywhere a world-wide "community of order."

> But in this world-wide community of order which the US is to dominate, all doors must remain open to "free (American) enterprise." All people must submit to American leadership and assume the role of subjects. To integrate into such a world economic imperialism is clearly to integrate into an American dominated economy which automatically means that other economic systems are reduced to inferior positions. For the world's peoples, the loss of an independent economy means the loss of political independence, as well as the loss of their own cultural personality.
>
> It is in the light of all this that we should examine American aggression in Vietnam. The policy of the Open Door to American Capitalism all over the world cannot fail to have as its number one enemy, the socialist countries. Socialist countries must, by definition, close this door to "free enterprise" and construct a solid barrier to capitalist domination. Given this fact, the main object of American policy must be to prevent extension of the Socialist zone. If the 1956 elections had been held in Vietnam, doubtless Ho Chi Minh would have been victorious; but the immediate and imperative aim for the US there was to establish a satellite state on the lines of Taiwan and South Korea. In other words, the US had to choose between two alternatives, a Socialist government in South Vietnam or another puppet state. Their choice surprised no one. But the puppets could not subdue the resistance of the people; the neocolonialists could not thwart the Vietnamese will to be free and independent. And during the years 1963–64 a new dilemma arose; the puppet regime was collapsing under the people's pressure, the war between the puppets and the people was being won by the people. The next choice for the

Americans was an acceptance of the facts or an all-out American war. Again no one was surprised, the choice was inevitable.

As I have already said at Stockholm, the underlying deeper reasons for this choice are not directly economic in the sense that the US has invested capital in that country that could justify intervention. Nor is it, in my view, strategic concern which merits this colossal expenditure. Even though the US pushes its military bases close to China, South Vietnam is not indispensable to them.

The American choice of intervention and war was and is—grounded on the fact that they are faced with a general revolt against American domination in the three continents where the people are rising in defense of their objective and true self-interests. The US could not avoid this show-down in South Vietnam and must win any guerrilla war.

But are they winning? Not merely is there no proof of this, there are signs of the opposite. In spite of the enormous disproportion between means, in spite of a concentration of firepower hitherto unknown in warfare, in spite of an incredible technological development of weapons of mass destruction, the American imperialists have suffered constant defeat. They have been defeated because the NLF and the DRV have retained the total support of the Vietnamese. Apart from the few mercenaries and collaborators, the overwhelming majority of the people support the struggle against the United States. Dr. Wulff, who has lived for years in Vietnam, and the American press substantiate this; there is no other explanation for the course of the war.

And now the Americans have another dilemma—defeat or Genocide. And since the most haughty imperialist in the world cannot face defeat, with cynicism and indifference they choose Genocide. And for this choice there is a historical precedent. When the American Indian failed to conform to the design, they too were exterminated.

The United States is still moving westward and the frontier is being pushed on over the Pacific, towards and into Asia—until the whole is transformed into an American colony. Those who resist are, in the imperialists' eyes, in the same obstructionist position as was the Indian, they oppose the will of God. They are of an inferior lesser race which stands in the way of the exalted. They must then be exterminated.

It is in this way that American expansionism has made them become aggressors; arrayed against other races and peoples. And it is the final solution of "escalation," which brings the Genocide on the people that refuse to submit. This is the political logic of the American Government, and it is against this logic which we must unite the people. Not only in the cause of humanity, not only in solidarity with the people of Vietnam, but in common defense of the common good. In affirmation of the right freely to choose a way of life in accordance with one's own conscience. A right which the NLF has inscribed upon its banner; a right for which they and the heroic Vietnamese people are fighting and dying every day.

VI. Summary and Verdict of Sessions

Summary and Verdict of the Second Session

The International War Crimes Tribunal met in Roskilde, Denmark, from November 20 to December 1, 1967, to continue the study of the questions on the agenda set during the constitutive meeting in London in November 1966.

A part of this agenda had been covered at Stockholm from the 2nd to the 10th of May 1967, which led to the first judgment, dated May 10, 1967. From this first judgment, it results that according to the tribunal:

*First, the government of the United State has committed aggression against Vietnam under the terms of international law.

*Second, there have been deliberate, systematic and large scale bombings of civilian objectives in Vietnam.

*Third, there have been on the part of the government of the United States of America repeated violations of the sovereignty, the neutrality and the territorial integrity of Cambodia.

*Fourth, the governments of Australia, New Zealand and South Korea have been accomplices of the United States in the aggression against Vietnam.

In the course of its Roskilde session, the Tribunal was to study the following questions:

*First, the complicity of Japan, Thailand, and the Philippines in the acts of aggression committed by the government of the United States of America.

*Second, the use of products and weapons prohibited by the laws of war.

*Third, the treatment of war prisoners.

*Fourth, the treatment of the civilian populations by the forces of the USA and those which are subordinate to them.

*Fifth, the extension of the war to Laos.

*Sixth, and finally, the Tribunal was to pronounce whether the combination of the crimes imputed to the government of the USA could not receive the general qualification of genocide.

A few days before the opening of the Roskilde session, the Tribunal renewed its appeal to the government of the USA in order that it might send a qualified representative who could answer in an authorized way to the accusations brought against it. The appeal, like numerous previous appeals, has remained without effect.

The Tribunal has heard the qualified representatives of the Democratic Republic of Vietnam and of the National Front of Liberation of South Vietnam as well as those of the Neo Lao Haksat of Laos and of Cambodia, and has heard the grievances that they have presented. It has heard numerous witnesses from the most varied countries, and in particular Vietnamese citizens from the North and the South who are war victims, and citizens of the USA having belonged to the American army in Vietnam.

It has heard the reports drawn up by the investigative commissions which it had sent itself to Vietnam, both in the DRV and in the areas controlled by the NLF, and the USA, as well as the reports of the investigative committees of Japan and of the Democratic People's Republic of Korea. It has studied numerous reports furnished by scientific and legal experts and by historians. Abundant documentation in photographs and motion pictures has been presented, as well as samples of weapons and products, accompanied by the results of experiments made in connection with these.

It is in a position to give the following replies to the questions which it has studied.

FIRST, complicity of Japan, Thailand and the Philippines:

- A. The American army, in utilizing the land, naval and air bases on Okinawa, in disposing of all of Japan for the movement of its troops, in taking advantage of Japan's highly developed technical capacity and abundant equipment for the repair of its war and merchant fleets and planes and for all kinds of supplies and equipment, has made Japan, with the complicity of its government, one of the essential elements of its strategic system in its struggle against Vietnam. As Mr. Stennis, chairman of the Armed Services Subcommittee of the US Senate, has declared, without the help of Japan, "operations in Southeast Asia would encounter serious difficulties." Already, during the Stockholm session, the Tribunal condemned the complicity of Australia, New Zealand and South Korea. Concerning this last country, the Tribunal received precise evidence that it was not only an accomplice to the crime of aggression, but that its army had committed war crimes. The Tribunal has not received information on this point as to the armed forces of the other accomplice powers.

- B. From the reports and documents furnished to the Tribunal, it is clear that the government of Thailand has afforded the United States diplomatic help, that it has offered it the possibility of setting up on its territory bases from which are launched the most murderous American air attacks against Vietnam. These bases are extremely valuable to the USA because they make it possible to bombard Vietnam under infinitely easier and more economical conditions, and with lesser risks for the pilots. Finally, the Thai government has completed its complicity by sending to South Vietnam an expeditionary corps, fighting directly by the side of the American armies. The complicity of the Thai government is likewise direct, as concerns the acts of aggression against Cambodia and Laos of which we will speak later.
- C. The government of the Philippines, whose politices are almost totally aligned with the policy of the United States, affords the latter the use of the bases which it has kept on the territory of the Philippines, after the accession of that

country to a purely formal independence. It is rightly that the Philippines have been qualified as a typical example of a state under the neocolonial domination of the United States. In addition, the government of the Philippines has sent troops to South Vietnam; this contingent is at present time two thousand men strong and it will undoubtedly be augmented.

SECOND, on prohibited weapons and products:

The Tribunal wishes to recall the uncontested principles of the law of nations, as well as those which were set down in the Hague in 1907, and with respect to which the legality of a weapon must be appraised; the principle of the immunity of the civilian population, the prohibition on the use of toxic products, the prohibition of weapons that may cause superfluous harm. It has attached a special importance to the Martens clause which appears in the preamble of the Hague Conventions of 1907, and according to which the law of war depends on the principles of the law of nations resulting from the usages established between the civilized nations, the laws of humanity and the requirements of the human conscience. It is in the application of these principles that the official manual of the American army (Department of the Army field manual) entitled "The Law of Land Warfare," published in July 1956, under the reference FM 27-10. By the Department of the Army, makes it an obligation for the campaigning armies not to use any kind and degree of violence not really necessary for military objectives and aims.

The Tribunal has already condemned in Stockholm the use of fragmentation bombs (CBU bombs and pellet bombs), which are by definition intended to strike civilian populations, being inoperative against installations or protected military men. It has been informed that the use of these weapons has become intensified and they have been perfected in the form of delayed-action bombs.

The Tribunal wants today to condemn:

- The wholesale and indiscriminate use of napalm, which has been abundantly demonstrated before the Tribunal.
- The use of phosphorus, the burns of which are even more painful and prolonged and have, in addition, the effects of a poison on the organism.

As for the use of gasses, the Tribunal considers that the failure of the United States to ratify the Geneva Protocol on June 17, 1925, concerning the prohibition of the use in war of toxic or similar asphyxiating gasses is without effect, as a result of the voting by the General Assembly of the United Nations (a vote joined in by the United States) of the resolution of the 5th of December, 1966, inviting all states to conform to the principles and objectives of the said protocol, and condemning all acts contrary to these objectives.

The scientific reports of the most qualified experts, which have been submitted to the Tribunal, demonstrated that the gasses used in Vietnam, in particular CS, CN and DM, are used under conditions which make them always toxic and often deadly, especially when they are blown into the hideouts, shelters and underground tunnels where a large part of the Vietnamese population is forced to live. It is impossible to classify them as simple incapacitating gasses; they must be classified as combat gasses.

The Tribunal has studied the current practice of the American army consisting of spraying defoliating or herbicidal products over entire regions in Vietnam. It has noted that the American manual on the law of war already cited forbids destroying, in particular by chemical agents—even those theoretically non-harmful to man—any crops that are not intended to be used exclusively for the food of the armed forces.

It has found that the reports of the investigative commissions confirmed the information, from both Vietnamese and American sources, according to which considerable areas of cultivated land are sprayed by these defoliating and herbicidal products. At least 700,000 hectares (about 1,750,000 acres) of ground were affected in 1966.

THIRD, on the treatment of prisoners of war:

The Tribunal recalls that prisoners of war must receive humane treatment, under conditions which are defined by the Geneva Conventions of 1949, which the United States had signed, and the terms of which it has incorporated in its own manual of the law of war. Tortures, mutilations and serious physical and mental coercion are not only prohibited but must be punished. The prisoner is entitled to life and to the medical aid that his state requires.

Numerous testimonies, both Vietnamese and American, were heard (among the American witnesses was a former soldier whose function for ten months had been to question prisoners from the time of their capture), and it was established that these principles are a dead letter for the Americans in Vietnam. The finishing off of the wounded on the battlefield and summary executions are frequent. Prisoners are thrown into the air from helicopters. Torture in all forms, by electricity, water, burns and blows is practiced daily. All the witnesses have confirmed that these practices always occur in the presence and under the direction of American soldiers, even when they do not themselves participate. These tortures are aimed at obtaining information or confessions. Medical care is systematically refused to the wounded and ill who refuse to speak.

Finally, in contempt of the provisions of the Geneva Convention, the prisoners held by the United States which is the detaining power within the meaning of this Convention, are handed over to the authorities of the so-called Saigon government, which engages in a dreadful repression accompanied by acts of torture, numerous examples of which have been furnished, including those in which women are frightfully tortured.

FOURTH, treatment of civilian population:

The Convention of the Hague of 1907, the Nuremberg and Tokyo judgments, the Universal Declaration of Human Rights, the 4th Geneva Convention of August 12, 1949, lay down the undeniable principle of the protection of civilian persons in time of war. The manual of the law of war of the American army includes as one of its parts the entire 4th Convention of Geneva, the binding character of which is undeniable.

The Tribunal heard: the testimony of three American veterans, and the report of the investigations undertaken by its investigative mission in the United States, some Vietnamese victims, the report to the investigative mission of the Tribunal in the areas controlled by the NLF (which has collected 317 depositions, the minutes of which have been put into its files) and an important witness, a citizen of the German Federal Republic (Dr. Erich Wulff) who has lived several years in South Vietnam. It considers that the following facts are established:

- First, in the course of raiding operations which take place both systematically and permanently, thousands of inhabitants are massacred. According to serious information from American sources, 250,000 children have been killed since the beginning of this war, and 750,000 wounded and mutilated for life. Villages are entirely leveled, fields are devastated, livestock destroyed, in particular the testimony of the American journalist Jonathan Schell describes in a startling way the extermination by the American forces of the population of the Vietnamese village of Ben Suc, and its complete destruction. Precise testimony and documents that have been put before the Tribunal have reported the existence of free-fire zones, where everything that moves is considered hostile, which amounts to saying that the entire population is taken as a target.
- Second, one third of the population of Vietnam has been displaced, and shut up in the strategic hamlets which are now baptized New Life Hamlets. The living conditions, according to published reports that have been brought to the Tribunal's attention, are close to those of a concentration-camp life. The interned—women and children in most cases—are parked like cattle behind barbed-wire fences. Food and hygiene are almost entirely lacking, which often makes survival impossible. The social structures and traditional structures of the Vietnamese families

are thus destroyed. One must also take account of the fact of the impressive number of prisoners held in the jails of South Vietnam—400,000 according to estimates that are worthy of attention. Arbitrary arrests, parodies of justice, interrogations accompanied by abominable tortures, are current practice. All the testimony agrees in establishing that inhuman and illegal methods are daily being used by the American armed forces and their satellites against the civilian populations, who are thus threatened with extermination.

FIFTH, on the extension of the war to Laos and Cambodia:

As a corollary of the American aggression in Vietnam, the security of the two neighboring countries is seriously compromised.

1. The Laotian people are plunged into war by the direct extension on their territory of American aggression. On the one hand, the violation of the Geneva Agreements on Indochina of 1954, like those of the Geneva Agreements on Laos of 1962, and the support given by the governments of the United States and of Thailand to the local pro-Amercian forces, constitute a blatant intervention in the domestic affairs of Laos, and have revived the war in Laotian territory. Moreover, military personnel of the United States and its satellites—South Vietnamese and Thai—have been introduced into Laos, Transforming the part of the territory controlled by the Vientiane administration into a military base in the service of American aggression, both against Vietnam and against the rest of Laos. Finally, American planes that leave from bases situated in Thailand regularly assault the Laotian population, accumulating deaths and ruins.
2. Cambodia as the Tribunal has emphasized in its Stockholm judgment, is the victim of repeated violations of its frontiers perpetrated by the armed forces

of Thailand and of the government of Saigon, in the pay of the United States. It is also the victim of repeated bombings, both aerial and artillery, from the American forces. The situation analyzed in Stockholm has only become aggravated, and the heaviest menace hangs over the Kingdom of Cambodia, as its Chief of State has pointed out to the Tribunal.

Therefore, the International War Crimes Tribunal, does as a result of deliberations, render its verdict as follows:

Is the Government of Thailand guilty of complicity in the aggression committed by the United States Government against Vietnam?
Yes, by Unanimous Vote.

Is the Government of the Philippines guilty of complicity in the aggression committed by the United States Government against Vietnam?
Yes, by Unanimous Vote.

Is the Government of Japan guilty of complicity in the aggression committed by the United States Government against Vietnam?
Yes, by 8 votes to 3.

(The three Tribunal members who voted against agree that the Japanese Government gives considerable aid to the Government of the United States, but do not agree on its complicity in the crime of aggression.)

Has the United States Government committed aggression against the people of Laos, according to the definition provided by international law?
Yes, by Unanimous Vote.

Have the armed forces of the United States used or experimented with weapons prohibited by the laws of war?

Yes, by Unanimous Vote.

Have prisoners of war captured by the armed forces of the United States been subjected to treatment prohibited by the laws of war?

Yes, Unanimous Vote.

Have the armed forces of the United States subjected the civilian population to inhumane treatment prohibited by International law?

Yes, by Unanimous Vote.

Is the United States Government guilty of genocide against the people of Vietnam?

Yes, by Unanimous Vote.

Dave Dellinger, an American pacifist and member of the Tribunal, had some closing remarks, an appeal to American and world opinion:

> Unlike the Nuremberg Tribunal which met after the crimes had been committed, the International War Crimes Tribunal is meeting and rendering its judgments at the very moment when the crimes are taking place and even being escalated. The Nuremberg Tribunal asked for and secured the punishment of individuals. The International War Crimes Tribunal is asking the peoples of the world, the masses, to take action to stop the crimes. At Nuremberg the accused rested safely in jail, and the main focus was on the past; our Tribunal is quite different. Unless the masses act, and act successfully, we stand only at the beginning of war crimes and genocide—genocide that could bring down the cites and destroy the populations of the world.
>
> No matter how horrible the evidence presented here, we stand at the threshold of even more horrible and extensive crimes, unless the peoples of the world act. Let me remind you that the

history of the war in Vietnam is a history of continuous escalation. When the United States has found out that it cannot defeat the enemy of the moment at the level of warfare of the moment, it continually redefines the enemy and expands the form of its aggression. I will not go into the history of this expansion, but I will remind you that it began with diplomatic warfare at Geneva and elsewhere; it went through the stages of political infiltration, the training of puppets, the organizing of counter-insurgency, the training and leading of massive Saigon troops, and finally, the commitment of masses of United States troops.

As the United States loses in its battle with one enemy, it takes on new enemies. And as it escalates its enemies, it escalates the weapons. As the American GIs, David Tuck, Peter Martinsen and Donald Duncan testified, they went to Vietnam to fight Communists, and they were disillusioned when they found out that they were fighting Vietnamese; that they were there to kill anybody from the population. Already as the United States is losing at the present level of warfare and claims that as a "Great Power" it cannot admit defeat and cannot withdraw from this criminal enterprise, Secretary Rusk is raising fears of the "yellow peril" in China. The state of mind that affirms napalm and pellet bombs and poison gasses as weapons, is the state of mind that can affirm nuclear warfare.

Many people in the countries of the world, especially the Western countries, are watching from the sidelines, as they watched Hitler. In the time of Hitler they said, "It can't happen here." And in the time of the United States aggression in Vietnam, they are saying, "It can't happen to our cities; it can't happen to our populations." But already their countries are subjected to the diplomatic warfare that began the attack on Vietnam. They are subject to pressures on their governments and their economies. The United States Special Forces are scattered throughout the world. The Vietnamese know that they have no choice, except to resist. In many other countries, particularly the Western countries, people think they have a choice still. But they have none; they must resist. Paradoxically, if Hitler announced his intention to wipe out the Jews, the photos and the reports of the atrocities did not appear in the daily newspapers or go into the living rooms in television. And if the democratic façade in the United States has prevented the American generals and presidents from announcing their intentions, perhaps even from comprehending them in their full intensity themselves, the same democratic facade allows some of the reports and some of the photos to appear in the American mass media. And the psychology becomes, "It's all right to do these things, because we are a democratic country as shown by the fact that we tell about them in the press." And at a certain stage, the psychology becomes, "because we admit that we are doing these things, we are not really doing them at all." In other words they do not call these actions by their proper name, and do not present them in their proper intensity.

But a democratic society can commit genocide, as is illustrated by the history of the United States. I need only remind you of what happened to the American Indians and the black people. If the people in the Western countries, in particular, underestimate the total and genocidal nature of the United States' aggression, there is something else which they underestimate also. And that is the ability of the Vietnamese people to resist. If they underestimate the inhumane nature of the United States' actions, they also underestimate the human nature of the Vietnamese resistance.

The legitimacy of the Tribunal has sometimes been questioned. Its legitimacy will be determined by the answer given to its findings by the peoples of the world. The people of the world must refuse to commit the crimes that have been documented here. They must refuse to be accomplices in these crimes. But it is not enough to stop here. In addition they must make positive acts to stop the crimes. The Tribunal appeals to the people of the United States to stop the monstrous aggression of the United States at its source. It appeals to the people of the United States to put an end to United States' genocide. And finally, the Tribunal appeals to all the peoples of the world to act in the name of humanity and in the name of solidarity with our Vietnamese brothers and with all other peoples whose lives and honor and integrity are threatened.

Bertrand Russell's Final Address to the Tribunal, December 1967:

> In declaring our conclusions today, we do not merely pronounce judgment on past events. We do more than report the criminal policies and actions of a government. Our function is not that of an historian. We have not studied and deliberated solely in order to preserve the truth about Vietnam for posterity. We must discharge a deeper and harder duty; we speak because silence is complicity, a lie, a crime. We expose in order to arouse conscience. We condemn evil in order to extirpate its causes. Our truth challenges mankind.
>
> What words can describe the evil we've discovered? The moral, legal, and political categories by which we are accustomed to judge human conduct are inadequate for these crimes. The term genocide truly encompasses the enormity of American crimes in Vietnam. I shall not repeat the catalogue of horrors which we have witnessed these past ten days; let me only say that it is nightmarish in its dimensions and vividness; we shall never forget it. We must permit no one to be innocent of these facts. Everyone should know them and every man must judge them.
>
> Morally awakened men, willing to act—only these are needed to end America's war. Despite technological innovations, the Pentagon must rely ultimately on its conscripts, just as every imperial power has depended on innocent men, acting out of fear, habitual conformity and total ignorance, to enact the slaughter of aggressive war. The American soldier does not differ from the ordinary conscript of the First World War. His obedience and patriotism are underpinned by profound unawareness of what he will be called upon to do. We must reach him and make him aware. We must build resistance in America to the continuation of the war. In every land we must make known the reality of Vietnam. We must develop massive campaigns against the complicity of any government which fails to condemn American Genocide in Vietnam. Even in the nations which have uttered clear condemnations of the aggressors, it is never impossible to

increase the concrete aid to those who are struggling for justice in Vietnam. We must mobilize every people on the basis of our findings and create an international resistance to the war.

The months ahead are crucial. American casualties have increased gravely, in direct proportion to the escalation of troop commitments. Tens of thousands of Americans will be killed this year in Vietnam. The United States is losing the war. The peoples of every continent are aware of this. The Pentagon spends more and more dollars in desperation—one million for each guerrilla killed. It unleashes all its might fiendishly, but the heroic partisans of Vietnam endure. They will go on so long as a single Vietnamese survives. Our duty is to stand with them. The most lasting barrier to genocide is the unity of all peoples to whom justice is more than an empty phrase, and courage an indispensable attribute of morality.

Our Tribunal leaves Denmark, therefore, armed not only with the fullest evidence of American war crimes, but with the knowledge that the final chapter of these crimes is still unwritten. We appeal to everyone the world over to redouble his efforts to end this barbarism.

After reviewing the Russell Tribunal volume, I remembered that a few years back (1995) Robert McNamara wrote and published a book *In Retrospect: The Tragedy and Lessons of Vietnam* on his memory of his part in the war as Secretary of Defense from 1961 throughout the end of 1967. I borrowed a copy from the library to see what he had to say.

In the last few months, McNamara had turned somewhat dovish, and he wrote that he advised Johnson to seek negotiations aggressively, and make whatever cuts in the bombing of the North, as necessary, to encourage such negotiations. This occurred just before he left his post as Defense Secretary to assume the presidency of the World Bank, under Johnson's all out approval. This was in November 1967.

The first session of the Tribunal had taken place earlier in 1967 in Stockholm, and the second session was underway as

McNamara left his post. Not once in his book does he make mention of the Russell Tribunal, or its findings. All the events reported in the Tribunal volume had taken place during McNamara's tenure in office as defense secretary, except what was reported of events in the Truman and Eisenhower administrations.

On February 17, 1965, Ike was invited to attend a two and one half hour meeting with Johnson and his advisers. During the meetings Ike stated that LBJ's first duty was to contain Communism in Southeast Asia. He approved bombing of North Vietnam and the introduction of as many as eight divisions of US troops if that proved necessary. He also suggested "we should pass the word that if the Chinese or Soviets threatened to intervene, that dire results (i.e., nuclear strikes) might occur to them."

On March 2, 1965, sustained bombing of North Vietnam began. Operation "Rolling Thunder," as the air program came to be known, had begun. It would continue for three or more years and drop more bombs on Vietnam than had been dropped on all of Europe in World War II.

On page 244, he reports that sorties against North Vietnam grew from 25,000 in 1965, to 79,000 in 1966, to 108,000 in 1967; and the tonnage of bombs from 63,000 to 136,000 to 226,000 respectively.

On page 321, McNamara reports the troop level of American forces in Vietnam and the total troops killed in action by that time. November 1963:16,300 advisors, 225 killed in action. Late 1964 or early 1965:23,300 advisors, 225 killed in action. July 1965:81,400 troops, 509 killed in action. December 1965:184,300 troops, 1,594 killed in action. December 1967:485,600 troops, 15,979 killed in action. January 1973:543,400 (peak in 1969), 58,191 killed in action by then.

Note the deaths in 1967 as McNamara and Johnson parted ways over what to do next (15,979) and the end total as America finally agreed to a cease fire in 1973, nearly 43,000 more American boys killed in action. If one of your sons or brothers was included in that 43,000 figure, think what might have happened if the Bertrand Russell Tribunal and its findings had been made completely public to the American people, through the news media. Would the "Mothers of America" have allowed our government to continue doing the things that had been reported? I doubt it! As Donald Duncan indicated in his report on training of Special Forces, it was a concern of the Special Forces trainers not to let it become public what the troops were trained and ordered to do, lest the "Mothers of America" find out and object.

McNamara has some fifteen pages towards the end of his book on the lessons of Vietnam. All things considered, they are irrelevant when one considers the aggressive nature of our conduct from the end of World War II on; especially the American-Diem program to prevent the Geneva Accords of 1954 from being fulfilled.

In an appendix at the end of his book, he expressed the same concern I have had since observing the results of one A-bomb on Hiroshima eight days after it happened, on August 14, 1945, from the right seat of a B-29. His concern was that in a nuclear war 100,000,000 (100 million) Americans would die in the first hour of the exchange. He doesn't speculate what would happen in the second hour, or the second day, or in the weeks that would follow. He recommends total reduction of all nuclear arms as soon as possible. Think of this: a 60-megaton bomb, which was in existence at the time of the Cuban Missile Crisis, would be 3,000 times as powerful and destructive as the Hiroshima bomb.

Back to the events that led to the eventual cessation of hostilities there in Vietnam. The news media essentially ignored the findings of the Tribunal while the sessions proceeded, and also after publication of the findings in early 1968 by O'Hare Books. However, every peace center and peace activist group throughout the country got copies and did what they could to promote the 660-page book and protest the war.

The NLF added emphasis to the war with the "Tet" New Year's offensive in 1968, which made headlines for the general public to see and read. Otherwise they remained oblivious to what Americans were doing to the people of Vietnam. By people, I mean human beings, not some derogatory designation like "Gooks," *untermenschen*, slant eyes, etc., including women and children—250,000 children killed by 1967 and 750,000 maimed for life.

Then there was exposure of the facts on the My Lai Massacre by Seymour Hersh, who now has just published a book on *The Dark Side of Camelot*. The My Lai Massacre got the attention of the general public in this country.

McNamara had commissioned a review of all aspects of the Vietnam war a few months before he left the Defense Department. It wasn't completed until 1969. Daniel Ellsberg came across the documents at the RAND Corporation in 1969. There were some 7,000 pages of the material. He discovered that the war had been accompanied by lies and deception. In 1971 he turned over one copy of the documents to the *New York Times*. After months of agonizing over what to do, on Sunday, June 13, 1971, the *Times* published the first installment of a projected series based on the "Pentagon Papers" as they were to be called. The Nixon administration fought any further publication via restraining order. That same week the *Washington Post* got a copy and likewise started a series. In just a few days, the matter went all the way to the Supreme Court, which after reviewing the issue, the court denied the administration's request for a permanent injunction—on June 30, 1971. The *Times* and the *Post* then continued their series, and the *Times* published a nearly 700-page book condensation on the documents, which sold over a million copies.

Then in 1972 there was a photo of a nine-year-old Vietnamese girl, running stark naked from a napalm raid on a village and pagoda where she had sought shelter. She had stripped her clothes off because her back was covered with burning napalm. You could see the smoke and flames of the napalm raid in the background of the picture. When taken to a local infirmary, she was not expected to live more than a day or two. A newsman saw to it that she was taken to a special hospital in Saigon that cared for napalm victims where she was treated and survived some seventeen reconstructive surgery operations. She is now living in Toronto, Canada, where she was interviewed for an hour-long program, titled "The Girl In The Photograph," that was shown on TV on the A&E channel on November 8, 1997. Two of her brothers and two of her cousins had died in that napalm raid.

All of these events and reports helped to convince a lot of the American people that we should get out of Vietnam. Perhaps more than any other was this photograph of the nine-year-old girl, and the story that went with it. The peace centers and activists in the colleges spread the word as much as possible on all these events.

But never to this day have the findings of the Russell Tribunal been covered in the American news media. The one grudging exception appeared after the My Lai massacre—that maybe Russell was on the right track with his efforts. Then nothing more on the subject. My *Encyclopaedia Britannica* dismisses the relevance of the Tribunal with this brief comment: (page 648 of Vol. 29, 15th edition, 1986) "Under the aegis of Bertrand Russell the United States was 'tried' for war crimes in Vietnam by a self-constituted tribunal that sat in Stockholm. That this was a judicial farce was demonstrated by the fact that the offer of a Swedish attorney to represent the United States was rejected by the court."

I will leave it to the reader to evaluate the relevance of the evidence that I have summarized in the foregoing chapters. First a question: Is it essential, or customary, or even allowed for the accused to have an attorney present in the Grand Jury investigative proceedings into an alleged crime? For that essentially was the function of the Russell Tribunal.

On July 24, 1997, an article appeared in our *Mail Tribune*, in Medford, Oregon, about a local surgeon who had just returned from Da Nang, Vietnam, where he led a four-person medical team to treat "children and adults with foot deformities so severe that he had only read about them in medical textbooks. Many of the problems are rooted in malnutrition, said Dr. Patrick Code."

I wrote to Dr. Code asking if he didn't consider the probability of the herbicides sprayed on Vietnam, especially "Agent Orange" being the cause. He was too busy with his practice, I guess, to answer. I suppose malnutrition can mean bad nutrition, such as poisoned or contaminated food stuffs, as well as lack of food.

My *Britannica* says Agent Orange was a mixture of herbicides used by the military forces during the Vietnam War. The substance contained about equal parts of 24-D and 245-T with variable proportions of "Dioxin." Exposure of laboratory animals to dioxin is associated with abnormally high incidences of abortions, skin diseases, and birth defects. Some persons have suffered similar disorders after returning to the U.S. from Vietnam and have claimed that their afflictions resulted from exposure to Agent Orange. Vietnam veterans brought a class-action lawsuit against seven herbicide makers that produced Agent Orange for the U.S. military. The suit was settled out of court, with the establishment of a $180 million fund to compensate veterans and their families for disabilities thought to be caused by exposure to Agent Orange.

Another article about a businessman who had been asked to take a team of doctors and nurses into Vietnam by Northwest Medical Teams. A bit of his comments is worth relating: "We gave care in clinics with no sanitation where children suffered hopelessly without medication. We delivered toys to a school for disabled children with Down's syndrome and birth defects *caused by Agent Orange*, which still permeated the water table.'' The article appeared in the *Oregonian* for December 2, 1997, and Jack Estes was the businessman referred to in the article.

"Rolling Thunder" had been going on barely two months when President Johnson gave a major speech at Johns Hopkins University on April 7, 1965, in which he outlined a $1 billion development plan for Southeast Asia, if the Vietnamese would give up their plans for independence. I listened on television and then prepared a scathing letter to him and delivered it to an Associated Press office in San Francisco, dated April 8, 1965.

Dear Sir:
I have examined your speech of last night, and I am not impressed with your apparent generosity.

The 400,000 or more deaths by military action in the Indo-China area of Southeast Asia since our support of the French colonial forces in that area began, would indicate that you would buy salvation for the deliberately premeditated murder of those people for $2,500 per head. This in itself is preposterous. And considering that you would deny them the further right to self-determination of their political and economic direction after all the blood of theirs that has been shed to accomplish their true freedom, your proposals are extremely naive to say the least.

Your proposal, and those of your predecessors, reeks of hypocritical concern and assistance on a grand scale for those areas of the world where the challenge to the hundreds of years old colonial-imperialism is seriously complicating matters—primarily; but no real solution for a positive and definite program to uplift the various underdeveloped nations and peoples above their age-old starvation and pestilence conditions, is anywhere in sight in your prattlings.

From your presentation, I can visualize a continuing caustic hard-shelled attitude extending infinitely into the future. Whatever future might remain—with the aim and goal of American interests, and therefore foreign policy, the exploiting of the resources of backward nations for private profit of American and other colonial investors an ever accelerating process.

China has no starvation today, or in any recent past! What about India, Latin America, Africa, the Arab states, etc.—all "Free World" areas? The Colonial-Capitalist states do not have the political or economic answers for these areas of the world. History proves this fact. It is said that 10,000 infants per day are dying of starvation in those areas. That is 60,000,000 or more in the length of time the American instigated and perpetuated Cold War has ensued. But it is scheduled to get worse. It is predicted that billions will die during the 1970s of starvation if the vast war expenditures are not diverted to helping those areas of the world to get onto their feet. And I repeat and emphasize from the record of some 6,000 years of history—the status quo does not have the key answer to the problem of what to do. Only the "New Song Sung Before The Throne" provides the method of breaching the gap and providing the future means of an everlasting kingdom. Get with it.

I maintain that a thousand times your seemingly generous offer of $1 billion would be more appropriate and even approximately justified; for the status quo to contribute to world development and organization. Spread out over several decades, it would not be any more confining than the $750 billion spent on defense over the past 19 years. And we could have the full employment and prosperity so very well possible in our country. And we could feel proud of our contribution thereafter, rather than plagued by our conscience to the extent that we beg to be put out of our misery—as your current foreign policy indicates.

Our nation is indeed that Babylon the Great so long ago prophesied by that great book that you so often refer to in your hypocritical mouthings. Your actions and those of your three predecessors are what are described therein in such thorough condemnation.

I am enclosing notes and a lecture on the subject of Vietnam that you should read, if indeed you really have an ounce of sincerity in your whole lying make-up.

                Sincerely,
                Elton R. Maas

A few days later, a Secret Service or FBI agent came by my home to ask me if I had any intention of trying to harm the president. I assured him that I didn't; I had a family to try to support. I was just speaking my mind about his Vietnam War policy. He went his way and I didn't hear any more from them.

In my estimation, there are some grave incongruities in our treatment of Vietnam since the war. Just this year the U.S. pressed for settlement of a $130 million debt that Vietnam allegedly owes us. They agreed to pay it beginning with a first installment of $8 million. The U.S. promptly gave recognition to their government and sent an ambassador to Hanoi.

According to official figures, the U.S. spent some $200 billion destroying and killing in Vietnam. The seven herbicide makers put up $180 million to compensate the crews that handled Agent Orange, and their families. In view of the reports of medical teams on birth defects, etc., in Vietnam; and since our government ordered the production and sprayed Agent Orange over vast areas of Vietnam, it seems to me that we owe them billions of dollars in compensation for the effects of Agent Orange alone, on the Vietnamese people and their croplands.

Another incongruity: I've been reading in the news about the International Monetary Fund advancing tens of billions of dollars to prop up collapsing economies in Indonesia, Thailand, South Korea, etc. Is the IMF only for propping up staunch anti-Communist entities? Is the World Bank also oriented only in that same direction?

In 1975 when we finally got out of Vietnam, our federal debt was only around $500 billion. Since then it has climbed to ten times that figure; over $5 trillion, which our taxpayers have to pay interest on into the distant future. We only hoped to balance the budget by 2002, not pay any of it off, or reduce it. The Cold War has had its adverse effects on all our futures.

Why have I stressed so strongly the Russell Tribunal and its findings? There are several reasons, the most important being that the American people as a whole have never been told of those findings, via the only means they pay attention to—in the newspapers and on TV.

Another reason is that Russell and his efforts to get our nation on its proper course are foretold by Daniel 7:9, 13, and 22 as the Ancient of Days; and the blessed one of Daniel 12:11–12.: 11. "and from the time that the daily sacrifice shall be taken away, and ('til) the abomination that maketh desolate set up, there shall be a thousand two hundred and ninety days. 12:Blessed is he that waiteth, and cometh to the thousand three hundred and five and thirty days."

It is generally understood that "days" in the Daniel prophecies actually mean "years."

Way back in the early 1960s, I acquired a copy of H.G. Wells's *The Outline of History*. In reading it I came across a report on Muhammad's last pilgrimage to Mecca one year before he died, and he made then a great sermon. Wells analyzes in part the words, "they established in the world a great tradition of dignified fair dealings, they breathe a spirit of generosity, and they are human and workable. They created a society more free from widespread cruelty and social oppression than any society had been in the world before" and "all sacrifice was barred to the faithful, no loophole was left for the sacrificial priest of the old dispensation to come back into the new faith."

So that's the date that the daily sacrifice was taken away—in A.D. 631. One thousand two hundred and ninety years later, Einstein received his recognition in 1921 for his theory of relativity—$E=MC^2$, the interrelationship between matter and energy. This led to the Manhattan Project, for development of the atomic bomb—the abomination of desolation and abominations of the earth, that Babylon the Great is foretold to be the mother of. Einstein the "father"—America the "mother."

Forty-five years later, in mid-1966 (June 30), the blessed one of Daniel 12:12, Bertrand Russell, called for a grand jury investigation or International War Crimes Tribunal into America's involvement and actions in Vietnam—the 1335th year after A.D. 631.

In early 1966 I prepared a one-page paper on my analysis of the above dating of the prophecy, along with several other prophecies, and their dating. Much like others who had foretold a certain date, but failed to recognize it when it occurred, I likewise failed to recognize the fulfillment when it occurred.

Not till I began reviewing the 660 pages of Tribunal evidence just this year, did I connect the Russell efforts with the prophecies. The voluminous evidence accumulated by the individuals and teams that were sent to Vietnam to get firsthand information, the ex-soldiers' testimony, reports, doctors and victims; and a look at the picture of Russell at the Tribunal's Organizational Meeting in London, on page 656. Only then did it dawn on me that Russell fit the description of the Ancient of Days in Daniel 7:9 "—and the hair of his head like the pure wool—." So I feel that Russell should be given great credit for his efforts, not denigrated for same as did the *Encyclopaedia Britannica*.

William Miller, of Adventist fame, did some research in the early 1800s and figured that the "2300" days of Daniel 8:14 began with the order to restore and rebuild Jerusalem, as reported in Ezra 7:12:26, the same as the reference in Daniel 9:25–26—457 B.C.

In 1844 Miller and his followers were out on the hilltops awaiting the "rapture" that the prophecy seemed to them to indicate.

Nothing happened; but there was no way that Miller could have known that at that time, across the Atlantic Ocean in Europe, Karl Marx had begun his work on the *Communist Manifesto*, which has troubled the wealthy interests of our world so deeply. The Socialist ideal that Marx proposed: "From each according to his ability; to each according to his work" to build up a nation and its society to the level where the ultimate Communist Ideal "from each according to his ability; to each according to his needs" would become workable.

In Daniel 9:25, there is a prophecy that seems to date from the same 457 B.C. date: "Know therefore and understand, that from the going forth of the commandment to restore and to build Jerusalem unto the Messiah the Prince, shall be seven weeks and three score and two weeks" (69 weeks or 483 days—years). If Jesus was born in 4 B.C. as is now believed, then he would have been about 30 years old in A.D. 27, at the time he was baptized by John, which fits quite closely with the prophecy.

The next paragraph left me searching for an answer, and I think I found it. "After three score and two weeks shall Messiah be cut off, but not for himself; and the people of the Prince that shall come shall destroy the city and the sanctuary" (62 weeks would amount to 434 years); A.D. 27 plus 434 years would take this to A.D. 461. Could it be that the protective spirit of Christ was cut off, or removed, from the church that he founded, whose new holy city was Rome, after Constantine recognized the Christian faith as the recognized religion of the Roman Empire?

There is reference that the people of the Prince to come would destroy the city. Genseric the Vandal crossed over from Europe to Carthage, built a strong force, crossed the Mediterranean Sea, and sacked Rome in A.D. 455.

The people of North Africa as well as Arabia became followers of the Islamic faith that Muhammad founded. Could Muhammad therefore have been the "Prince to come," as foretold by Daniel? The Islamic faith did spread all across Africa and into Spain to the west, and to India, Indonesia, and the Philippines to the east—while Europe degenerated into the "Dark Ages" for centuries.

H. G. Wells remarked that at the time of his writing *The Outline of History* that the Islamic faith comprised some 300 million adherents, a truly major religious element in our world.

Hence the date of A.D. 631 and the reference point of the daily sacrifice being taken away, and 1,335 years later, on June 30, 1966 Bertrand Russell called for an investigation into America's acts in Vietnam.

One last thought on the above. In Luke 1:26–38, Mary is told by the angel Gabriel that she would conceive a child who would be called the Son of the Highest. In Daniel 8:16 and Daniel 9:21, there is reference to the angel Gabriel informing Daniel what is to come. The Islamic faith also lists Gabriel as the angel who informed Muhammad what to write and what to do.

VII. Some Bible Prophecies and Events That Relate

I am thoroughly convinced that Daniel 2:44, Daniel 7 for the most part, Daniel 12 completely, Revelation 14, 17, 18, and 19, and part of Revelation 16 pertain to this century, and are all interrelated with each other, and with historical events of this twentieth century. I hope I can adequately explain my understanding to you, the reader.

The first verse of Daniel 12 seems a good place to start: "And at that time shall Michael stand up, the great prince which standeth for the children of thy people; and there shall be a time of trouble, such as never was since there was a nation even to that same time; and at that time thy people shall be delivered, every one that shall be found written in the book."

The Jewish people of Europe experienced the "holocaust" in which some 6 million of them died. Since then, the remainder founded a nation of their own, Israel, and, perhaps through "divine" help, have managed to defeat the armies of Egypt, Syria, Saudi Arabia, etc., each time their new nation has been threatened.

There are three references to sealing the book till the time of the "end," with one of them concluding with, Daniel 12:4:"—many shall run to and fro and knowledge shall be increased." That fits well with our transportation systems of today, and surely knowledge has been increased by leaps and bounds in this century.

In Daniel 12:5–7, there is reference to the same "time, times and an half" that appears in Daniel 7:25; only in this Daniel 12 case, the one "upon the waters of the river" shows intent to "scatter the power of the holy people." If the saints of the Most High are the holy people therein referred to, then it seems to indicate an effort against God's Kingdom, just the opposite of that indicated in Daniel 7:25. Suppose, for an instant, the "river" mentioned here consists of the whole Atlantic and Pacific oceans. At the time of Daniel and up until 1492, the American continents were completely unknown to the peoples of Europe and Asia. Hence one residing on this North American continent would seem to be standing over the great "river."

Every presidential Administration since World War II has striven to contain and/or destroy the power and influence of the Communist nations. They have succeeded in breaking up the Soviet Union, the one nation that almost single-handedly stopped the mightiest army ever to be assembled in history, composed of all the nations of continental Europe, and drove them back whence they came. America still threatens Communist China with ever newer nuclear submarines and missiles.

In Daniel 7:13–14, there is reference to "one like the Son of man" who is given a kingdom, the same as in Revelation 14:14–16, "One like unto the Son of man," who is told to "reap the earth."

Daniel 2:40—43 gives a prophecy about the fourth kingdom on earth. Daniel 7:7, 19, 23 gives a prophecy as to the conduct of this fourth kingdom, or beast, in conquering the world, and the treatment of the native people overrun in the process. The European nations, particularly, Spain, France, Great Britain, Belgium, Holland, Italy, Germany, and to a lesser extent others, did indeed take over most of the world for their colonial empires, and subdue and mistreat the native populations. The European settlers of North America gained their independence from England in 1776–81 and proceeded to treat the Native Indians even more brutally than did other nations of the beast in their conquests, as the immigrants from Europe moved here and needed ever more land to reside on. The Indians were pushed onto reservations, "concentration camps," over the next 150 years; and the United States, "the little horn" of the fourth beast (Daniel 7) became the most powerful of all those nations of the fourth beast. *Reader's Digest* published a book a year or so ago, *Through Indian Eyes*, that covers the treatment of the Native Indians since the first "White Men" landed.

And according to Daniel 2:44, "In the days of those kings shall the God of heaven set up a kingdom," as the Christian adherents have been praying for for nearly two thousand years: "Thy kingdom come, thy will be done in earth as it is in heaven."

As a result of World Wars I and II, those European nations lost their direct domination over vast areas of the world that they had held onto for hundreds of years.

Now back to the "one like the Son of man" connection between Daniel 7 and Revelation 14. This reference places events in the same time frame, which I'm convinced is the twentieth century.

However, before the "reaping" could take place, the message of the "angel with the everlasting gospel" had to have time to spread to a particular portion of one country at least, as it spread to all "nations and tongues and people."

In Revelation 14, there is mention of 144,000 from the twelve tribes of Israel, who would learn the new "gospel" (according to Mark) before being reincarnated onto the earthly plane. These were the "*first*" redeemed unto God and the Lamb" (way back in the first century or so A.D. we could guess) and would follow the "Lamb" whither-so-ever he goest. This ties in with the thought in Revelation 17:14, "and they that are with him are called, chosen, and faithful."

There is mention of Babylon in Revelation 14:8:"Babylon is fallen, is fallen, that great city, because she made all nations drink of the wine of the wrath of her fornication."

This ties in with Revelation 18:23:"—for thy merchants were the great men of the earth; for by thy sorceries were all nations deceived—" and with Daniel 7:25:"and he shall speak great words against the most High."

America has been broadcasting the Voice of America, Radio Free Europe, and Radio Free Asia out over the airwaves for a couple of generations, or more, and all of it to disenchant the people of the world from Communism. Some of what they broadcast no doubt has a grain or two of truth in it, but most of the stuff is mostly distortions, exaggerations, and many even outright lies. Hence the above references to America as Babylon the Great, and the "little horn" of Daniel 7.

There is also reference to the beast. In Revelation 16:13–16, we see reference to the Battle of Armageddon instigated by the dragon, the beast, and the false prophet. I feel certain that Germany, Italy, and Japan of World War II are represented by these three, which would mean Armageddon was World War II and the three Kings of Daniel 7: subdued by the "little horn" were the same Axis powers of World War II. Revelation 17 gives the most credit to the Soviet Union for stopping Hitler (the beast), but America was deeply involved in winning the war against all three of the Axis belligerents of World War II.

I have suggested that the United States of America is the "Babylon the Great" of the Revelation prophecies, as well as the "little horn" of the Daniel 7 prophecy. Let's look at some of the other evidence that would indicate that conclusion in Revelation 18.

Revelation 18:3:"For all nations have drunk of the wine of the wrath of her fornication, and the kings of the earth have committed fornication with her, and the merchants of the earth are waxed rich through the abundance of her delicacies."

Perhaps the reference to abundance was my first clue. Technocracy had taught me that abundance was America's problem that led to the Great Depression of the 1930s; how to efficiently distribute the great amount of our production to our people under a pricing system.

The Fascist-leaning nations of Western Europe joined Hitler in the attack upon the Soviet Union in 1941, and together they fought the dirtiest war in history, trying to destroy Communism at its source. The USSR lost 20 million of their military age men in driving the German armies back out of their land. Vast destruction of their land and facilities also occurred. Some 8 million or so of their other people were also killed, especially if they were suspected Communists or Jews. By contrast the United States lost only some 400 to 500 thousand soldiers in all areas of combat; and no destruction of our productive facilities occurred other than what was destroyed in the attack on Pearl Harbor.

After the war America began to help rebuild Western Europe through Marshall Plan aid and formed an alliance with those nations that had helped Hitler fight the dirtiest war, in the North Atlantic Treaty Organization (NATO) in effect, challenging the spread of that economic ideology that Hitler had tried so hard to destroy. Later when South American and Asian countries leaned towards Communism, our CIA and Special Forces stepped in and helped overthrow them and/or strengthen the anti-Communist elements of those countries. The most tragic example of this was our support for Suharto in his overthrow of Sukarno in Indonesia. An estimated 1 million people were massacred by Suharto's forces throughout the land. (I have a pamphlet on that 1965 event entitled "The Silent Slaughter," with an introduction by Bertrand Russell.

Then of course, there were Japan, South Korea, the Philippines, Thailand, Australia, and Taiwan, which cooperated with the U.S. in the Vietnam War. Hence the reference to them being "harlots" (Rev. 17:5) and committing fornication with Babylon the Great.

Revelation 18:7:"How much she hath glorified herself, and lived deliciously, so much torment and sorrow give her; for she saith in her heart, I sit a queen, and am no widow, and shall see no sorrow."

America has indeed glorified herself, and lived deliciously, and one of the prime objectives of the nuclear arms buildup over half a century is to protect ourselves through the threat of massive retaliation in case we are attacked. It could also be called nuclear blackmail against any nation that might decide to threaten our interests anywhere in the world.

For a long time, I worried that we might be destroyed in a nuclear war, for the words of Revelation 19:3—"and her smoke rose up for ever and ever"—would seem to indicate nuclear radiation and its half-life.

In mid-1960 an article appeared in our San Jose, California, paper saying the USSR then had 50,000 nuclear bombs and missile warheads; but never fear, we had twice as many, or 100,000. It was later estimated by several analysts that 100 million Americans would be killed in the *first hour* of a nuclear war with the Soviet Union.

But after the Soviets chose to point their missiles away from our direction, I have been concerned about another possible cause of America's (Babylon the Great's) destruction. Perhaps some of you have been following the stated scientific concern over a near-earth asteroid or comet striking America, or some part of the world, as supposedly one did that destroyed the dinosaurs off Yucatan some 65 million years ago, or perhaps you saw the made-for-television movie *Asteroid,* which was shown on TV in 1997. There are two prophecies that might well indicate that scenario.

> [Revelation 18:21] And a mighty angel took up a stone like a great millstone, and cast it into the sea, saying "Thus with violence shall that great city Babylon be thrown down, and shall be found no more at all."

[Revelation 10:7] But in the days of the voice of the *seventh angel*, when he shall begin to sound, the mystery of God should be finished—(There is just one stated mystery in the Bible, that I know of; and that is who Babylon the Great is.)

[Revelation 16:17–21] And the seventh angel poured out his vial into the air; and there came a great voice out of the temple of heaven, from the throne, saying, It is done.

18:And there were voices, and thunders, and lightnings, and there was a great earthquake, such as was not since men were upon the earth, so mighty an earthquake, and so great.

19:And the great city was divided into three parts, and the cities of the nations fell; and great Babylon came in remembrance before God, to give unto her the cup of the wine of the fierceness of his wrath.

20:And every island fled away, and the mountains were not found.

21:And there fell upon men a great hail out of heaven, every stone about the weight of a talent; and men blasphemed God because of the plague of the hail; for the plague thereof was exceeding great.

There were several movie plots of recent years depicting an asteroid impact on earth. One movie, *Doomsday Rock*, starred actress Connie Sellecca and her father as the heroes after her father deciphered some drawings found in a prehistoric cave in Australia. These drawings depicted an asteroid colliding with a comet, causing the asteroid to be diverted to a collision course with earth at a specific time. The father and a crew hijacked a missile silo complex in the Southwest to get control of nuclear missiles to destroy the asteroid. The government took Connie to Washington, D.C., to get her to reason with her father to give up. Eventually she gained access to a telescope and actually watched the collision occur. The government was ready to blow up the missile complex—hostages, hijackers and all—but Connie persuaded them to stop the attack just in time. Her father obtained the necessary details for launch control in time to save the world.

In *Deep Impact,* a seven-and-one-half-mile wide asteroid was headed for earth. An astronaut crew was organized to intercept the asteroid and drill a 100 foot deep hole in the asteroid and place a nuclear bomb in it and try to blow it up. They succeeded in breaking it into two chunks. One chunk, one and one-half miles wide, was going to descend into the Atlantic Ocean and create tidal waves as high as 3,500 feet. The six-mile-wide chuck was due to impact in Canada and create a so-called "nuclear winter" for several years. The astronauts heading back to earth and learning the results of their failure determined to fly into the larger chunk with four other nuclear bombs aboard and sacrifice their lives in an effort to blow up that larger chunk—which they did and saved the world from a catastrophe like the dinosaurs experienced sixty-five million years ago. Still, millions died on the shores of the Atlantic from the giant tidal waves.

The plot of a blockbuster movie released last year, *Armageddon* had some elements of sense to it, but a lot of unreality also. A crew of oil-well drillers were enlisted to train as astronauts, in order to drill an 800-foot deep hole into a Texas-sized asteroid that was headed for Earth. A nuclear bomb would then be lowered into the bottom of the hole so it could explode after the astronauts/drillers were a safe distance away. The time element involved in the task was unrealistic, as was the obstacle course they encountered once they landed on the asteroid. The accomplishment of splitting the asteroid in half so that each half would pass the earth on opposite sides was highly improbable. The task of one individual, Harry Stamper (played by Bruce Willis), to impel the nuclear bomb eight hundred feet down the hole, and proceed with it clad in a spacesuit so he could trigger the explosion manually, since the remote-triggering mechanism had been damaged en route to the drilled hole, was the most unreal part of all, but there was a lot of drama in the story, and even a love-story element as well.

I wonder sometimes if these plots don't offer the viewer a false sense of security—that whatever comes at us, the government, or someone, will save us from the impending catastrophe.

Another recent plot (TV's *Asteroid*) had it due to impact near Kansas City, Missouri (the home of President Truman, who started the Cold War on April 22, 1945, weeks before Germany finally surrendered, and further stepped it up with the Truman Doctrine a few years later). It is of interest that the Mormons (Latter-Day Saints) have a prophecy that some thing would wipe clean a huge section of western Missouri, and thereafter they would build the "New Jerusalem" on that devastated area of land.) But vehicles carrying laser weapons were sent up to divert its course, and Dallas, Texas, ended up as the major impact point. Perhaps as a result of the breakup of the asteroid, many parts of the earth had smaller pieces of the asteroid impacting on their cities and countryside. So it would seem that movie people as well as scientists are considering the possibilities of such an event. And two Revelation prophecies seem to me to foretell just such an end to our Babylon the Great.

Earlier I tied Daniel 7:25, "And he (the little horn) shall speak great words against the most High" together with Revelation 18:23, "For thy merchants were the great men of the earth; for by thy sorceries were all nations deceived" and remarked on how Voice of America, Radio Free Europe, and Radio Free Asia fit into this prophecy. One of the major concerns at the present time in our country is the source of campaign donations and the means used to solicit same. Large wealth interests supply the bulk of all campaign funds. Likewise the news media depend mostly on advertising revenue for their ongoing operations, and the thrust of the news that is regularly available to the public is potentially biased towards what the wealth interests approve of; and I am certain they have exercised that power a great deal during the Cold War period. Do we have a true democracy? Or do we in fact have what might be called a plutocracy, in which some truth reaches the public, but not nearly to the extent that it should?

And then there is the last verse of Revelation 18:"And in her was found the blood of prophets, and saints, and of all that were slain upon the earth."

Before proceeding with an explanation of the above responsibility of America for so many deaths, I want to point out that I began getting the picture of America as "Babylon the Great" nearly fifty years ago in the fall of 1948. I spent a lot of time and money during the 1960s trying to get my analysis of events in relation to Bible prophecy in front of all the congressmen, senators, and presidents of that time. In 1964 I ran off a thousand copies of my analysis (ten typewritten/mimeographed pages) and distributed them around the Santa Clara Valley, where I was living and working at Lockheed, Sunnyvale, at the time. One paragraph commenting about some "boondoggling" at Lockheed cost me my job. I was told I was not allowed to criticize my fellow employees. I had worked for first Burbank Lockheed from 1951 to 1957, and at Sunnyvale till I was dismissed in the fall of 1964.

My next major effort to publicize my findings was in 1976 after we had moved to Central Point in the Rogue Valley in 1970. My wife of thirty years died in 1974 and I felt I could afford a more expensive effort to reach my fellow Americans and Christians. I prepared a 45-page booklet of my analysis and had five thousand copies printed. I then prepared a full-page ad in the local *Mail Tribune* prior to the primary election, and a two-page spread in the same paper just before the general election.

Very little came of it, so the next year when I was invited to join the International Platform Association (IPA), I joined and attended their convention in Washington D.C. in July 1977, and came away with an idea to advertise in their *Talent* magazine. Over the next two years, I placed five informative, full-page ads at an expense of around $500 apiece.

On April 17, 1980, I wrote a letter to President Carter, and submitted it also as a sixth ad for *Talent* magazine. At the time of my writing, there was a hostage crisis in Iran, where a large number of embassy personnel were held hostage by the Iranian government.

A LETTER TO CARTER

Dear Sir:

No doubt you are aware of my analysis that America is indeed that "Babylon the Great" of the Revelation—from my ads in *Talent* (IPA) magazine, from my letter to your concerned wife shortly after "Toccoa" and my letters.

It does, perhaps, seem strange that an American who fought in World War II in a B-29—thirty-five combat missions over Japan—could think of his country as such a criminal entity as foretold, especially considering the final condemnation of Revelation 18:24:"And in her was found the blood of prophets, and of saints, and of all that were slain upon the earth."

Let me assure you that this is not an idle accusation. We tend to blame Hitler, Mussolini, and Tojo for the massive death and destruction of World War II. My evidence indicates that it was the "rich men" of our 20th century that set those men up in power—some from America, some from Japan, some from Germany, and some in Italy and other European nations—whose greatest desire was to destroy this threat to their uncontrolled power over human affairs that the Bolshevik-Marxist revolution represented. The same type and caliber of "rich men" that the Trilateral Commission of today consists of.

In World War I these "rich men" waxed richer through their munitions contracts and their manipulation of the tides of war, to reap the maximum profit therefrom. But they recognized the threat to their money power that the Russian Revolution represented, and soon brought to an end the brutal war in Western Europe. It was not long though before expeditionary forces from

Britain, France, and America made an attempt to end this Bolshevik threat; 1918–22 saw the "Western Intervention" in Russia and Siberia. When this proved too unpopular and/or costly, the "Allies" settled for what they had carved out of the Russian nation and went home. Poland, Estonia, Latvia and Lithuania, in part at least, were formed from the captured territory.

Then in the winter of 1932–33 the "rich men" were shocked to their boots by a new version of the "Communist menace" achieving widespread publicity and approval right here in America. The new idea was based on a pair of fictional best-sellers published a few years before the turn of the century: *Looking Backward—2000–1887 A.D.* and *Equality* by Edward Bellamy of Massachusetts. Some news media carried extensive coverage on "TECHNOCRACY" for months. Those more in the "know" remained aloof with a wait-and-see attitude.

When Howard Scott was invited to speak to the greatest assemblage of financial wealth under one roof at the Hotel Pierre in New York City and told "them" that there was no place for a financial superstructure in a Technocracy, little doubt remained. Technocracy "died" quickly in the headlines of the advertiser dominated media—and Adolph "Schicklgruber" rapidly achieved the financing he needed to advance to a position of supreme power over Western Europe. During the Spanish Civil War, the duly elected government of Spain couldn't get so much as a Chevrolet truck from America, but Franco, backed by Hitler, Mussolini, and the Vatican, got all the war materials he needed, much of it from America, transshipped via various South American countries, and Hitler had his proving ground for his "Wehrmacht."

Suppose America would have recognized the true moral character and merits of Edward Bellamy's works; and early in this century have instituted his design here in America. Would World Wars I or II have ever occurred? Would the Bolshevik Revolution even have developed? No, none of this bloodshed would have ensued.

If those wealth interests had only accepted "Technocracy" and not run scared after Hitler in 1933, there would have been no Spanish Civil War or World War II.

Had America remained friendly to our fightingest ally of World War II and settled the affairs of the world as recommended by one of your Southern Christians, Edgar Cayce "The Sleeping Prophet," none of the strife of the Cold War period—Korea, Vietnam, etc.—would have occurred. None of the torture and murder of tens of thousands of Vietnam and Iran, and a million Indonesians under Suharto murdered, would have happened. The multiple trillions of dollars of wasted effort and resources that have manifested in the armaments race since World War II could have been much more appropriately spent on uplifting the third world nations—instead of holding them in subjugation to the Capitalist exploitation that they continue to endure.

But even this is not the worst of the picture of the misdeeds of "BABYLON THE GREAT" (America).

A prophecy of Jesus speaks of the great judgment day, when He shall say, "Verily I say unto you, Inasmuch as ye did it (did it not) to one of the least of these, ye did it (did it not) to me" (Matt 25:40–45). Keep this in mind!

A little over a year ago, our *Mail Tribune* editor reported in an editorial relating to the "population bomb," an estimated 20,000,000 (20 million) children are dying of starvation and malnutrition around the world each year!

Now we know that in the major Communist countries, China and the USSR, great emphasis is placed on education, health, and of necessity nutrition for the children of their realm, so that starvation of the children cannot be taking place there. It has to be still occurring in the remaining third world that America, Capitalist exploitation thrust, is still keeping in subjugation to an outmoded and decrepit colonial system! In fact, America has, with its armies and influence, replaced all the old colonial powers of Europe and Japan in a unilateral guarantee of continuation of access to exploitation of these third world nations by the old powers, and by and for America itself. We have become the supreme colonial power of this generation.

Even if we figure half the estimated child starvation rate—spread over the thirty-five years since the end of World War

II only—the figure comes to 350,000,000 (350 million) children starved to death, in the interests of continued capitalist domination of those areas, just since we could have most recently taken the proper course in world affairs!

In 1966 Bertrand Russell prepared a plea for an International War Crimes Tribunal against the U.S. for its criminal actions in Vietnam. The news media of our Western Bloc nations, especially America, ridiculed the efforts of Lord Russell and/or summarily ignored it. The Tribunal did eventually take place, and America was found guilty on numerous counts. Not until the My Lai Massacre hit the headlines did any American media show any respect for Russell's efforts, and then only momentarily, until the lid could be clamped down again.

We now come to the current Iranian crisis, over the embassy hostages. You say there is nothing for America to apologize to Iran for? The *60 Minutes* program recently covered the matter of the Shah, Rockefeller interests, and CIA involvement quite enlighteningly. The *Spotlite* newspaper had shown the picture from a different angle, relating to tens of billions of dollars of rip-off. A book written by Prof. Reza Baraheni, who spent 102 days in the Shah's torture chambers, *The Crowned Cannibals*, gives an inside look. One particular episode horrified me no end: (p. 174–75) ''—A little girl, scarcely six years old, had been placed in front of several men in handcuffs. My interrogator is there. Hosseini, the professional whipper of the Komite, asks the girl questions about the identity of these men. The girl is having difficulty understanding what the torturer is talking about. She is beaten on the face, and her ears and hair are pulled. When the questions are repeated, the girl is terror struck. Hosseini beats her again. This goes on for some time until one of the men in handcuffs can stand it no longer and gives away his identity. The girl is taken back to her cell. The man is taken to the third floor torture chamber—''

You still say there is nothing for America to apologize for??? The CIA supported and trained these torturers, as they did the Diem regime during the 1950s, who tortured and murdered some

70 to 80 thousand Vietnamese—solely because they signed petitions for the elections they were promised in 1956, but were never allowed to have, because "Ike" felt that the people would vote 4 to 1 for Ho Chi Minh and the North Vietnamese regime.

The news media ignored and ridiculed Bertrand Russell. They are up against a more demanding news situation in the Iran-Hostage crisis. They cannot ignore it, much as they would like to. (The recent *Doonesbury* cartoon of an alleged conversation between you and the keeper of the Rose Garden elucidates their feelings.) The true situation is gradually seeping into the consciousness of the American people. You are forced, as President of these United States, to come to grips with the realities of the situation. Yet you still hesitate to admit to the wrongdoing of our nation, and its leaders. How can you continue to harden your heart?

If the Shah got away with some $28 billion as accused, surely the Rockefeller interests must have acquired as great an amount, if not several times more. The great agri-business operations that were set up in Iran, and more recently in Brazil according to a recent *Bulletin of the Atomic Scientists* report, are not designed to help the people of the involved country, but rather is yet another means of exploiting the land, resources and people of the country, for the benefit of the financiers of the operation, and for the people of the old colonial powers where the agri-business production ends up. The agri-business is even dangerous ecologically, according to the *Bulletin*.

Yes, America has failed to rise to its responsibility many times; at the turn of the century after Edward Bellamy had lit the way for our country; after World War I when we fought the Bolsheviks in and around Murmansk, and were lined up to fight them near Vladivostok, but didn't; when Howard Scott's TECHNOCRACY exploded into the news in 1932-33, but the "rich men," who control the media through advertising, opted for Hitler, instead; after World War II when we could have remained friendly with the USSR; after the Vietnam War when we could have become thoroughly aware of the evils and wrongdoing of our leadership; and now in relation to the hostage crisis in Iran—where our nation's misdeeds there, on the world scene, have again been brought into the limelight. Can't you see that America must repent—apologize—and change???

Yes, America is that "BABYLON THE GREAT" of the Revelation; and the judgment cannot be far off. Whether it be the destruction of the West Coast of California as predicted for the 1980s by Edgar Cayce & others (see *We Are the Earthquake Generation* by Jeffrey Goodman, Ph.D., Seaview Books) (Revelation 16:18–21), or by Nuclear Holocaust, likewise seen by many prophets, and Revelation 18:& 19:1–3. There is a very good reason why so little time is left. The resources humanity is needful of are so rapidly being depleted in the armament race and in other hoggish and wasteful processes of the industrialized nations of the West. If the USSR should gain control of the oil rich resources of the Middle East, it would serve Japan and the Western Gentile nations right.

Why don't you apologize to Iran, and return the Shah and his misappropriated billions of dollars to their rightful owners—the people of Iran—as a first gesture of our admission of long-term guilt on the whole world scene???

Think of the 350 million children who have died of starvation just since World War II. You may be called to account for them—or the even greater number who will starve by 2000 A.D., if you fail to change our nation's course.

Sincerely,
Elton R. Maas

President Carter received this letter in his mail on April 20—the abortive rescue attempt of the hostages was April 23—Leland Jensen, a Bahai Faith interpreter of prophecy, made nationwide publicity for his prediction that America would be destroyed by a nuclear holocaust on April 29, or in a few weeks thereafter—May 2. Dan T. Moore, Board Chairman of the International Platform Association, turned down this ad for the June issue of *Talent* magazine, as having "too many highly controversial and arguable statements in it." One wonders at the "fine threads of chance" that our civilization hangs on.

On May 15, I gave up trying to get the IPA to reconsider, and arranged for a reprint on the back of my fifth ad, which was printed in March 1979, and which I had had some thousand copies printed. That ad was titled "Nuclear Age and War."

Three days later, on May 18, "Mother Nature" exploded—a big chunk out of Mount St. Helens. Considering my analysis of the Bible prophecies, particularly Daniel 2:44 relating the Communist-Bolshevik revolution in Russia to that prophecy for the God of heaven to set up a kingdom on earth; the next paragraph, Daniel 2:45, "For as much as thou sawest that the stone was cut out of the mountain without hands," etc., may well relate to the Mount St. Helens explosion.

On June 1, 1980, Eric Allen, our *Medford Mail Tribune* editor, had the following to say. (Reprinted with permission of the *Mail Tribune*, Medford, Oregon.)

Mount St. Helens & H-Bombs

In the continuing story of Mount St. Helens and its current series of eruptions, one thought obtrudes. Scientists have estimated the total force of the mountain's first major blow-out was close to that released by a hydrogen bomb.

What if, instead of a natural volcanic occurrence, it HAD been an H-bomb? Nearly 100 people are dead or missing as a result of the volcanic eruptions, but had the event been a hydrogen bomb explosion, the death toll would have been thousands of times greater.

The ash from the mountain is mildly radioactive, but no more so than most rocks. The fallout from a hydrogen bomb explosion would be fatally radioactive. And as the ash from the mountain covered most of eastern Washington thickly, and less so elsewhere, radioactive fallout from a bomb would have caused death or illness over a huge area of the United States.

Those who believe that nuclear war is "thinkable" might ponder on Mount St. Helens's lesson for a few moments.

On May 30, columnist Art Hoppe had a pointedly tongue-in-cheek article relating to Mount St. Helens also. (Copyright 1980 *San Francisco Chronicle* Publishing Company. Reprinted by permission of the author.)

A Heavenly Blast

SCENE: *The heavenly Real Estate Office. The Landlord is happily hanging a dozen brand new stars in a brand new galaxy. His business agent, Mr. Gabriel, enters, Golden Trumpet in hand.*

THE LANDLORD *(singing):* A couple of jiggers of moonlight and add a star—

Gabriel: Excuse me, sir, I have a final report at last on that experiment you wanted conducted on that little planet Earth.

The Landlord: Ah, yes, the tiny jewel I love so dearly. How did it go, Gabriel?

Gabriel: A complete failure, I'm afraid, sir.

The Landlord (frowning): What? Didn't the volcano go off?

Gabriel: Oh, yes, sir, right on schedule. Their president, himself, flew over the scene and reported in awestruck tones the devastation and desolation the disaster caused.

The Landlord: And who got the credit, Gabriel?

Gabriel: Oh, everyone agreed it was an act of you, sir.

Landlord: Yet they didn't understand why I did it?

Gabriel: To tell you the truth, sir, no one asked. Really, it's unbelievable, what with all the hints we gave them.

The Landlord: Hints, Gabriel?

Gabriel: Oh, yes, sir. We had their own scientists tell them the explosive force of the eruption was equal to one good-sized 50-megaton thermonuclear bomb.

The Landlord: What other clue could they possibly need? Wait, did you forget the fallout?

Gabriel: Of course not, sir. Their newspapers published maps showing a broad swath of fallout extending all the way across the continent. And there were photographs of streets and highways buried half a foot deep in the stuff.

Landlord: Well, what did they say about that?

Gabriel: They said it fouled up their automobile engines and might cause some cosmetic damage to their apple crop.

Landlord: By me, Gabriel! Didn't they wonder what would have happened had that fallout been radioactive?

Gabriel: Well, they did test it to see if it was poisonous. And I suppose they were relieved that it wasn't.

Landlord: But they missed the whole point, Gabriel. Here I go to all this trouble to demonstrate clearly to them exactly what horrible damage a single nuclear bomb could wreak. And they don't grasp the warning. Why, I suppose their leaders didn't even sign that Strategic Arms Limitation Treaty.

Gabriel: No, Sir. Instead, they voted to decrease the money they will spend on the poor in order to increase the money they will spend on new weapons (*raising the Golden Trumpet*). Shall I sound the Eviction Notice now, Sir?

Landlord: No, Gabriel. I see no point in doing for my creatures what they seem bound and determined to do for themselves.

As a follow-up to the above comments from Art Hoppe and Eric Allen, I feel it pertinent and appropriate to quote that "Nuclear Age and War" ad from the March issue of IPA's *Talent* magazine in 1979.

Nuclear Age and War

For days I have been wondering and stewing on just how to write up this ad for *Talent*. Today as I was about to commence,

I received my January issue of *The Bulletin of the Atomic Scientists*. The issue was filled with articles on the problems of our Nuclear age. Inside the front cover were two paragraphs I must share with you, for it was a joint appeal of Albert Einstein and Bertrand Russell in 1955 that these were taken from.

> There lies before us, if we choose, a continual progress in happiness, knowledge and wisdom. Shall we instead, choose death, because we cannot forget our quarrels? We appeal as human beings to human beings. Remember your humanity and forget the rest. If you can do so, the way lies open to a new paradise; if you cannot there lies before you the risk of universal death.
>
> In view of the fact that in any future world war nuclear weapons will certainly be employed, and that such weapons threaten the continued existence of mankind, we urge the governments of the world to realize, and to acknowledge publicly, that their purposes cannot be furthered by a world war, and we urge them, consequently, to find peaceful means for the settlement of all matters of dispute between them.

Scientists from both East and West responded to this appeal, and the Pugwash Movement was born. For twenty-two years, eminent scientists have met, without publicity, to work toward lessening the danger of nuclear war. Out of these meetings have come the SALT talks, the Partial Test Ban Treaty and the Non-Proliferation Treaty.

The Bulletin itself was founded in 1945, the year of Hiroshima (which I myself witnessed the remains of on our final combat mission of the war, minutes before the word came over the Armed Forces Radio that Japan had agreed to surrender. I was a B-29 pilot. We had just bombed the Marifu railroad yards, and instead of turning for home as soon as the bombs were away, our squadron kept on in the direction of our bomb run. Soon we saw why, as a town of ashen remains appeared ahead of us. We all agreed that it would have taken five hundred B-29s, loaded with conventional bombs, to do as thorough a job.) Albert Einstein, J. Robert Oppenheimer, Harold C. Urey, and some thirty other outstanding scientists were co-founding sponsors of *The Bulletin*.

The magazine's symbol, the "Bulletin Clock," stands at nine minutes to midnight, a symbol of the threat of nuclear doomsday hovering over mankind, and how close it might be in the event of nuclear war.

For thirty-four years now, *The Bulletin* has repeatedly emphasized the pall of mutual suicide that hangs over our world, and which, for the most part, our people blindly ignore.

Bertrand Russell is now gone from the world scene, and Albert Einstein is said to have uttered with great remorse as he lay dying, "I have destroyed the world," for it was his communication to FDR that led to the Manhattan Project, the atomic bomb, Hiroshima, our nuclear arms race, and—oblivion for mankind if the tide cannot be turned from its course.

As long ago as the fall of 1960, I knew that we were rapidly approaching the point of total destruction of all human life on the earth, and I knew that the passage from our Christian Bible specifically pointed to that danger: Mark 13:19–20:"For in those days shall be affliction, such as was not from the beginning of the creation which God created unto this time, neither shall be. And except that the Lord had shortened those days, no flesh should be saved."

I even had notice two weeks ahead of time of the danger of nuclear war occurring on October 5, 1960, although most of our nation didn't know until the April 1961 *Reader's Digest* came out with its lead article "You Are Under Attack; The Strange Incident of October 5th"—a chance for shortening the days?—and I also knew in October of 1962 that Mark 13:14, the first paragraph of that theme was specifically pointing to the Cuban Missile Crisis, when President Kennedy made such a fuss over those medium-range (500-mile) missiles and that they shouldn't be there. They allegedly upset the balance of power. Mark 13:14:"But when ye shall see the abomination of desolation, spoken of by Daniel the prophet, standing where it ought not (let him that readeth understand)—"

President Kennedy lied to us all, deliberately, when he said those missiles specifically brought all our major East Coast cities under nuclear threat from Castro's Cuba. A 500-mile missile from Cuba's launching platforms couldn't have reached beyond the borders of Florida—you can check it for yourself on any world globe or map of that area. The farthest Florida Key was ninety miles from Cuba, yes, but even the southern border of Georgia was well out of reach of those missiles.

The danger to our major cities was not from Cuba, but from the ICBMs that were for a long time operational and based somewhere in the USSR, in the event that our nation really pressed the issue of Cuban missiles, and a mutual compromise could not be reached. Then that "too late" holocaust would have occurred in which "no flesh should be saved."

You may doubt this, but think for a minute. By the beginning of the 1960s, the United States had some 100,000 warheads ready for use, ranging up to a thousand times as powerful as the Hiroshima bomb—and the USSR had at least half as many, some up to 50 or 60 megatons of TNT in destructiveness. How many cities in America can boast of 100,000 or more population? One Hiroshima bomb can destroy anything of less population. That was nineteen years ago, so just imagine what the nuclear arsenals amount to by now! *Reader's Digest* for July 1976 had a rundown on a small part of that arsenal—just those stationed in nuclear missile carrying submarines. If you failed to get the import of that article, your local library should have a copy.

I knew the seriousness of those two moments in our history, before the October 5th incident, and as the situation developed in October of 1962, something only one was to know, according to Jesus in Mark 13:22:"But of that day and that hour knoweth no man, no, not the angels which are in heaven, neither the Son, but the Father." You will note that He did not place the Father in heaven as he did the angels, or as He did in the opening of the Lord's Prayer. Would you say that Jesus was a liar, mistaken, or—??? I prefer to think of Jesus as abhorring the telling of any lie.

Most of the time, our news media have ignored, turned a deaf ear to, the dangers of our nuclear age—but on January 14, our local newspaper editor broke through the cone of silence on the matter. His editorial, comparing the atomic weapons to the great equalizer of the nineteenth century, the Colt 45, is indeed a rare gem of enlightenment. (Reprinted with permission of the *Mail Tribune*, Medford, Oregon.)

The Equalizer

In the 19th Century, when the west was being won, the Colt revolver won the nickname of "The Equalizer," because when armed with one, the smallest and weakest man was potentially the equal of the largest and meanest when it came to a showdown.

Now that the nuclear club is as large as it is, and with the prospect of growing to include almost any two-bit nation with a few engineers and some weapon-grade uranium or plutonium, one wonders if we're not in another era of The Equalizer.

The threat of nuclear war has kept the two super-powers, the US and the USSR, from hostilities for nearly thirty years (although there were a couple of near things).

The US and the Soviet Union between them have enough lethal megatonnage to wipe each other off the map several times over and have the delivery systems to do so, from land, the air, and beneath the sea. Each has known that a nuclear war would be unwinnable—and probably unsurvivable.

But the awesome facts of a nuclear holocaust have been with us so long that they tend to be pushed into the back of the mind.

And this has permitted, even abetted, a continuing arms race that is ultimately futile and potentially fatal.

All the Strategic Arms Limitations Talks in the world are not going to halt the arms race until there is mutual recognition that a nuclear war is another name for mutual suicide.

Unlike Colt's revolver, the "equalizer" of atomic weapons is an equalizer only in the sense that it puts everyone in equal danger, and any atomic shoot-out at the OK Corral would take the whole neighborhood with it—the neighborhood, in this case, meaning the civilized world as we know it, and very likely the uncivilized parts too.

It is the great tragedy of the human race that it cannot foresee the consequences of its actions, or if it does, it lacks the power to change directions before it is too late.

If we survive into the 21st Century, it will be as much by luck as by any reasoned approach to peace as practiced by the nations, great and small, today.

In the midst of the worst of the Cuban Missile Crisis, I sent the following telegram to President Kennedy.

Sir:

It is my sincere belief that the USSR is indicated by Rev. 14:14, and that China is indicated by the 17th verse. I also believe that the 18th chapter of Revelation accurately describes the United States as it appears today in the eyes of God. I sincerely recommend the solution to our problems long proposed by Technocracy.

                    Sincerely,
                    Elton Maas

I never knew whether this telegram made any difference, or whether anyone ever read it. But in early 1975, I was given a booklet about Violet Gilbert, a psychic medium who was one of those quoted in Jess Stern's book *The Psychic Lives of Taylor Caldwell*. On the last two pages was allegedly a message from

Jesus, the Christ, June 20, 1967, through Violet Gilbert. One thought struck me in the middle of the message that seems to verify that we have already passed the danger of Mark 13:"—and if it had not been for the grace of the one God, there should not remain upon this planet, flesh." Another: "It is true, in learning to use the cosmic energies in their God nature, that some of the systems went through war-like conditions but never to the extent that has been expressed upon your planet Earth. And now, in the greater stages of development, it would be impossible to express the war-like nature of your planet. It is true that even the most high patience can be tried and rather than being a weakness, it becomes necessary to participate and to play the game, so to speak, as you would do."

And again we see a hint of the presence of God the Father here on earth, in a position to watch and change events. Violet Gilbert gave another hint of this in the *Psychic Lives of Taylor Caldwell*, in which she said, "—in time to come, very near in the future, there will be the attempt from the *most high* to bring the world of light unto man again—"

If you were to read in Luke 1:26–35, you would see that Mary was told Jesus would be called the Son of the Highest, or as some Bibles translate it, Most High. If you were to look up God, names of, in a good *Jewish Encyclopedia*, as I did around the early 1960s, you would find the name *Elyon*, translated "Most High," the ancient name for God back in Abraham's day, so now you know what name to "Hallow" when you recite the Lord's Prayer. But I have been told on good authority, that the modern spelling of that name is Elton. When I wear the rainbow button "Elton for President," I am literally saying, "I am tired of what the politicians, and their backers, are doing to our World. I want God to take over and run this country, just like we were taught to pray for in the Lord's Prayer."—"Thy kingdom come, Thy will be done, in (on) earth as it is in heaven," symbolizing that desire to the best of my ability. Why don't you join me in this effort???

The original "Nuclear Age and War" ad had the button emblem at the start of the article, in black and white. On the thousand reprints, however, I had it printed in full color, with the rainbow showing red on the interior, next yellow, with greenish blue on the outside—as you would see formed around the sun at certain times, through high cirrus clouds. I got the idea from Revelation 10:1:"And I saw a mighty angel come down from heaven, clothed with a cloud, and a rainbow was upon his head, and his face was as it were the sun—10:2:and he had in his hand a little book open," which John is later told to eat up, sweet as honey in his mouth, but bitter in his belly.

I had a little "Elton for President" booklet of forty-five pages printed in the spring of 1976, and as I wrote it up and proceeded with the effort, I had great expectations about it, sweet as honey. But so little came of several thousands of dollars spent on the effort to enlighten my fellow citizens, you might say that it turned bitter.

The emblem was prepared at the same time as the booklet, after seeing a brilliant rainbow around the sun one day.

The booklet consisted mostly of a letter that I wrote to Charles Colson, of Watergate fame (?) who, while in prison for his part in it, got religion and commented in an article in the "Family Weekly," a Sunday supplement to our *Mail Tribune*, that "Without God we (our nation) will fail." This was March 28, 1976. I began writing the letter that same day and finished it the next.

In the letter I referred to a prediction made by a Bishop John Koyle of Salt Lake City, in what was jokingly called the Republican Elephant Dream, for a four-year drought and crop failure during the then-current, 1976, Republican Administration. He had the dream in 1930, and it was reported in C.T. Buchanan's "Full Gospel Native Missionary" for October 1975.

In my letter I wrote, "If you will note of California's winter drought; the dust bowl conditions of the early 1930s reenacted in Kansas and other parts of the Midwest; and a report from an area of Arkansas, that they had only one (1) inch of rain since last summer—then you can realize that the situation has already begun."

Perhaps the "powers of heaven," "Mother Nature," whatever, had high hopes for my efforts also; for no sooner had I finished my letter, on March 29, than the drought broke with a series of tornadoes in Arkansas, and by April 25, the whole Midwest was in receipt of two to four inches of rain.

Back to something current: On February 4, it was on the news that Yeltsin, Russia's leader, warned of a possible escalation to world war, if the United States attacked Iraq over the problem of United Nations inspectors not being allowed to go certain places in that country to inspect for weapons of mass destruction. In view of Einstein's and Russell's warning, which I had just finished typing for this manuscript, I felt it necessary to again avert catastrophe with a letter to President Clinton, if possible. I sent a telegram that night to the president. "I would give serious pause for thought over whether to proceed with an armed attack on Iraq that might trigger a world war. Letter Follows."

The next day I sent the following letter, along with the "Nuclear Age and War," "A Letter to Carter" ads, and a four-page letter addressed to college program chairmen and boards dated June 7, 1980, analyzing the Mount St. Helens explosion.

President Bill Clinton:
Dear Sir:

I received your letter of Jan. 19, 1997, thanking me for the material I sent.

I don't know if the enclosed material was included or not, but in case not, I am enclosing a copy that might prove pertinent to the present Iraq, Saddam Hussein, confrontation.

Both China and Russia oppose your threat to attack Iraq. Yeltsin, in the news today, worried that it might lead to a world war. In my "Nuclear Age and War" ad (enclosed) of March 1979, in *Talent* magazine; I quoted a joint appeal of Albert Einstein and Bertrand Russell, which reads in part. "In view of the fact in any future world war nuclear weapons will certainly be employed, and that such weapons threaten the continued existence of mankind, etc.—"

The United Nations members who are pushing for a military strike against Iraq showed little concern over America's violation of the UN Charter, the 1954 International Agreements on Vietnam, or the murder of some 6 million Vietnamese citizens, and the vast destruction of their land and facilities.

You know that I consider the Russian, Bolshevik, revolution as the fulfillment of the promise of Daniel 2:44 for God to set up a kingdom on earth, of His ideals.

The next paragraph speaks of (Daniel 2:45) "a stone cut out of the mountain without hands—" Perhaps that was the Mount St. Helens explosion. (See my June 7, 1980 letter, enclosed also.)

There is another prophecy in Revelation 18:21 that seems to tie in with Revelation 16:17–21, which I called to your attention in my earlier letter accompanying the material which you thanked me for. Revelation 18:21:"And a mighty angel took up a stone like a great millstone, and cast it into the sea, saying, Thus with violence shall that great city Babylon be thrown down, and shall be found no more at all." What a waste!!!

I would give serious pause for thought over whether to proceed with an armed attack that might trigger a nuclear holocaust!!
    Sincerely,
    Elton R. Maas

P.S. What was the basis of that 130 million dollars that Vietnam allegedly owed the United States before we would recognize their country and its leadership?? I've been trying to find out from my congressman, Bob Smith.

In November 1998, I wrote a letter to the *Mail Tribune*. My letter was published on Thanksgiving Day, November 26, 1998, and copies were sent to President Clinton and UN Secretary General Kofi Annan.

November 11, 1998

Editor, The Mail Tribune:

For some 9 or 10 months, since the agreement on inspections of Iraq's weapons facilities was brokered by Secretary General Annan, the inspections have been proceeding quite well—without any reciprocity on the *easing of sanctions* forthcoming. Is that fair? I can appreciate Iraq's impatience with the net results of the agreement.

On a recent answer and question item on a *Jeopardy!* program, Iraq was indicated as the one referred to in the Revelation 18 prophecy as Babylon the Great. I suppose because that was where the original Babylon was located. Is this the thinking of the U.N. and American leadership?

But the truth is that the United States of America is the entity described so accurately in Revelation 18, for its instigation and pursuit of the Cold War. Not Iraq, but the United States is the World Bully that is trying to run the world for the benefit of the wealth interests of the world using its near monoply of nuclear weapons as "nuclear blackmail."

If the current military threat that is being considered against Iraq is carried out, I hope it doesn't backfire into a world conflict—with nuclear weapons employed.

Sincerely,
Elton R. Maas

VIII. Equality

In science, when something is observed that does not fit the normal pattern or rule of things, it is called an *anomaly*.

Perhaps I could be called an anomaly, and my analysis of the world and its events in relation to the prophecy likewise an anomaly.

The Communists officially deny any relationship to religion, and so did Technocracy. Both maintain that the ultimate goal is to have a workable economy of abundance, where all can share equally in that abundance—with no extremely rich nor any poor and destitute, on the basis of scientific reasoning and planning.

Science has been a thorn in the side of religion ever since Charles Darwin's *Origin of Species* was published. Since then astronomy, geology, and archaeology have proven that this old earth, its sun, and most stars and galaxies have been around a lot longer than since 4000 or so B.C., which is the fundamentalist view of the creation story.

Four to five billion years is now the estimated age of our solar system and earth. Light from some distant galaxies has been shining our way for some 10 to 20 billion years.

Working with simple but sophisticated "lie detectors," called "E meters" in Scientology, practitioners claim to have discovered "memories" of lives that were lived as much as 60 trillion years ago in another universe, and of a giant spaceship, or city, in space. Arscylcus, that traveled for some 10,000 consecutive lifetimes across space, between universes before arriving in this one. They have some tall tales, or recollections, of events they have experienced since arriving in this universe as well.

But back to my analysis of the Bible, prophecies, etc., I do not question the scientific evidence of geologic records, the theory of *Origin of Species*, and the evidence acquired from astronomy. Yet something occurred around 4000 B.C. as related by folklore (word of mouth) that had to do with Adam, Eve, Cain, Abel, and Seth. Perhaps the Most High, as God was called in the Canannite society, or some angel of note, gave the information to the early people who managed to put it down in some form of writing for posterity. Now according to Genesis 4:16–17, Cain, after being sent away, found himself a wife in the land of Nod, had children, and built a city named Enoch, after the name of his firstborn son. So there had to be other human life on the earth prior to the Garden of Eden story.

I have wondered that the "flood" story, with Noah as the hero, might have had something to do with the earth having a huge cloud cover prior to the flood, somewhat like Venus currently has, but with a surface temperature compatible with living things, and the rainfall finally opened up that cloud cover to the point where the sun shone through—and for the first time a rainbow was seen, or was it a reverse bow as can be seen from time to time around the sun when it shines through high cirrus clouds, as described in Revelation 10:1. This last is purely conjecture, of course.

What I'm trying to get to is this: we don't know everything there is to know about heaven or earth. It seems to me, however, that many prophecies of the Bible are quite accurately being fulfilled in this century. If the previous six thousand years are preliminary to the thousand-year millennium, or millennial age, then we are on the verge of that prospect.

In Daniel 12:4,9, and 13, there are three references to the end times. What will it be the end of? Will it be the end of human life on the earth, as would occur as a result of a nuclear holocaust? Would it be the same or similar result if a huge asteroid, or comet, were to strike, somewhat like the event that occurred off the

Mexican Yucatan peninsula some 65 million years ago, which scientists now believe destroyed the dinosaurs? Or could it be the end of the rich man's, corporate, control over human affairs? Whatever might happen, I do sincerely believe that the Daniel 12 prophecies pertain to this twentieth century.

I am well aware that America's corporate enterprise system has made great strides in production techniques that have made possible an abundant life for our nation. However, some of this rich life that we enjoy has come about as a result of exploiting the resources, cheap labor, etc., of other parts of the world. Also, to protect this economic system, we have spent great sums of money, trillions of dollars, to prevent other nations and peoples from adopting and developing a system that is contrary to our private enterprise system. If my analysis of Bible prophecies is anywhere near correct—against the establishment of the Kingdom of God on earth, worldwide.

This brings me to mention a book that I have in my library. *The God That Failed*, edited by Richard Crossman. It consists, after an introduction by the editor, of the stories of 6 ex-Communists who became disillusioned by the "Party Line" dictates of the Stalin leadership in Russia. There is no mention in the stories, or in the introduction, of the accomplishments of the Soviet armies stopping Hitler's "*wehrmacht*" at the outskirts of Moscow, Leningrad, and Stalingrad—and then pushing them back to Berlin, and then surrounding and capturing the German capital while American and British forces were still some distance away.

The introduction and every one of the stories is related as if Hitler had finished the job that he had set out upon, or as if the stories were written in early 1942, before Stalin and his forces began to drive the German armies back where they came from—even though the book was first printed in 1950 by Harper & Brothers, and reprinted by Bantam Books in 1952, long after World War II was over. All of the six writers had hopes and expectations that they were working for the "Kingdom of God" in their joining and efforts for Communism.

In my opinion it was the very "Party Line" dictate of Stalinism that was the critical factor that led to the total defeat of Hitler and his temporary European helpers; Revelation 17:14:"These shall make war with the Lamb, and the Lamb shall overcome them, for he is Lord of lords and Kings of kings; *and they that are with him are called, chosen, and faithful.*"

The "Lord of lords" title pertains to the Stalin position of power as First or General Secretary of the Communist Party in the Soviet Union; and the "King of kings" title relates to the position of Premier of the Union of Soviet Socialist Republics.

Whatever the propagandists have to say about Stalin's purges and elimination of opposition during the 1930s, the above prophecy clearly points to that battle against the invasion of the Soviet Union by Hitler, as accurately as could be seen from 1,900 years earlier, and definitely indicates Stalin as the Lamb.

Hitler, and those other European leaders who held power with him for "one hour," were intent on destroying Communism, per se. The US of A took over the task from Hitler on April 22, 1945, even before the German surrender on May 10. Harry Truman threw down the gauntlet with a violent verbal attack on Molotov, while he was on his way to San Francisco to participate in the formation of the United Nations. He stopped off to pay his nation's respects to the new president—and got the Missouri Mule Driver's treatment by Truman. Then the "Truman Doctrine" became official a couple of years later.

Recently, on a history program of the final stages of World War II in Europe, on the History Channel, it was stated that the Soviet troops lost some 28,000 soldiers in the final assault on and capture of Berlin. Earlier on another history program, it was reported that the USSR lost 20 million killed in driving the German armies out of their land, and another 8 million Russian civilians were killed by Hitler's armies as they advanced.

As long ago as 1959, a *Population Reference Bureau* analysis of the population figures and ages of Soviet people, indicated that 20 million figure of military-age people killed in the war.

There is one more element in relation to prophecy that is about World War II. After Hitler's invasion, Stalin reversed the emphasis of his powers in order to gain the utmost support from all the Soviet peoples for his battle with the "beast"—Hitler. In Revelation 19:16, it reads, "KING OF KINGS, AND LORD OF LORDS" and is emphasized just like that, in capital letters, in my King James Version of the Bible.

There is yet another book, published in 1939 and topping the non-fiction best-seller list for many months from 1939 through 1941. The book, *Days of Our Years*, tells of the travels and observations of a Dutch writer, Pierre Von Paassen, between the wars.

He covers the horrors of the Spanish Civil War, where Catholics were fighting on both sides, but that the papal hierarchy was firmly behind Generalissimo Francisco Franco and his invasion—the same as Hitler and Mussolini were.

In one chapter he tells of meeting and conversing with a Swiss minister, Leonhard Ragaz, who confided in him that he believed that the Russian Bolshevik experiment was the Kingdom of God being established.

Von Paassen also reports on the Munich conference in 1938, when Czechoslovakia was dismembered by the agreement between Chamberlain and Daladier on one side and Hitler and Mussolini on the other—and strongly condemned that agreement.

During the 1960s, I came across a monthly newsletter from Australia by a Reverend C. P. Bradley, *United People*. Each issue consisted of ten pages of short paragraphs on his observations of world affairs. Following are a few paragraphs from the April 1967 issue that are pertinent to the theme of this book.

10. LBJ to Vietnam: "For peace, there must be equal moves on both sides." Equal? Does that means that Vietnamese men

must rape millions of your young women? Equal? Then the Vietnamese would spread VD all around the USA, blow down hundreds of schools and hospitals, kill many hundreds of school children, doctors, nurses and patients? Equal? By Valhalla, LBJ; you talk a lot of stupid nonsense!

When Svetlana, Stalin's daughter, left Russia, Bradley had this comment:

21. "Probably, Svetlana, more lies have been told about your father than about any man in history—perhaps that is the highest compliment you could pay any man."
63. JESUS TAUGHT BROTHERHOOD OF MAN. That was HIS GOSPEL—the gospel of the Kingdom of God. No church today has the courage to teach that. Teach that, and you come into violent collision with men of great economic and political might. That is why no one dares to teach "THE BROTHERHOOD OF MAN," and why ALL CHURCHES JUSTIFY THEMSELVES BY *CHARITY* WORK.
64. Some may think that my writing is severe, yet I believe anyone would write as I do, if they saw the world as I see it. The history of mankind is depressing. As "UNITED PEOPLE" said in our first issue, here: "The white races and the Christian church are drifting into an unspeakable disaster." I dare believe that, perhaps in a small way, I may help to prevent that shocking disaster. I AM AMAZED AT THE COMPLACENCE OF THE CHRISTIAN CHURCH. To listen to the clergy preaching sermons, one would think that there is nothing wrong with this world.

Going back to World War I era, I learned in Technocracy that one Howard Scott participated in a national study of production capabilities of the United States to find out if our nation could effectively produce the necessary munitions and equipment to launch an expeditionary force to Europe to aid the British and

French in defeating Kaiser Bill's armies. The study indicated we could—easily.

As an outgrowth of this study, and in conjunction with the studies of Thorstein Veblen, who had studied Edward Bellamy's books, they and their coworkers formulated an idea that became known as Technocracy, with Howard Scott the head of a continent-wide organization.

Earlier I related how Technocracy reached a wide audience in the news media in the winter of 1932–33 and was quickly silenced when it was learned that business, finance, and politics would have no place in a Technocracy. Science, technology, and engineering would be the guidance in the new system. Technocracy—science applied to the social order.

Scott estimated that America could produce such an abundance of all things that every adult could have the equivalent of $20,000 per year per adult, in 1929 dollars, and only have to work four hours per day, for four days per week, from age 25 to 45 and be retired at full income after 45 for the balance of life, and be educated till 25—free.

About the time of that short-lived publicity, as many as 21 million potential workers were idle and looking for work, and factories were closed down and/or working at a low level of production.

The nation never really recovered until the war effort of World War II stimulated the economy.

Quoting from a 1946 publication of Technocracy, "The United States in the year 1944 consumed 35,707 trillion BTUs of extraneous energy. This is the all-time high of energy consumption by any nation in history. This consumption is at the rate of 180,000 kilogram calories per capita per day. Canada reached its all-time peak of 140,000 kilogram calories per capita per day in the same year. It was this terrific consumption of energy that enabled the United States to maintain over 14 million of its most able-bodied citizens in its armed forces, and at the same time export billions of dollars of Lend-Lease to the other Allied nations around the globe.

This all-time high of energy consumption not only equipped, maintained and supplied the Armed Forces of the United States, and produced and transported the vast volumes of Lend-Lease, but at the same time produced the greatest quantity of consumer goods ever consumed by the American people per annum. This huge production of war goods, physical plant and equipment, and consumer goods became possible only because the United States possessed the resources, the technological equipment and the engineering skill to achieve it.

The United States and Canada in five years of World War II mobilized their respective armed forces, and organized their huge technological production while coordinating their national effort, politically and economically, for the collective attainment of a common goal—military victory. This military victory cost over $300 billion and over 300,000 lives.

These two nations could with equal facility mobilize their manpower, their machines and their money for a physical and economic rehabilitation that would be an investment in the future of a continent and its people. An efficient expenditure of $300 billion under a technological control would banish toil, poverty and disease from the face of this continent. Let every citizen of this Continent ponder this well. The peoples of Canada and the United States have it within their power to impose their will upon the conduct of human affairs just as easily as they acceded with patriotic fervor to the demands of a war economy.

Science or physical knowledge is being ushered in as the third order of knowledge in the affairs of men. The two other orders of knowledge have dominated mankind until today but it becomes imperative that they be relegated to their proper positions and that the conduct of human affairs be dominated by science, the physical knowledge of the world in which we live.

In the passing of the old and the instituting of the new, human conflict will become the bitterest in history. Science is hated and feared by ecclesiastical institutionalism, by corporate enterprise and political parties. The fear and hatred that will be directed by these against science and its technological applications will be far greater than those the Inquisition hurled against all the accumulated heresies. Only science and its technological application to the means whereby we live can produce for mankind the control of his social destiny here on this earth.

Now about the $300 billion that could have done so much for our country and people under a scientific or technology management—that Technocracy recommended. It is of great interest to me that in the first 200 years of our country's history, including all the wars we have waged, and even the $200 billion spent on the Vietnam War, the total federal debt had risen to barely half a trillion dollars ($500,000,000,000) by 1976. The next twenty years have seen our federal debt multiply ten times over, to over $5 trillion, all of it requiring interest to be paid on it by a large portion of our yearly taxes.

Some of that increase might well have resulted from the welfare programs that have been intended to help the poor, but there are still a lot of poor, and great quantities of homeless in our nation. The politicians and their bosses, the Capitalists (the rich men), just don't have the solution to our problems. Most of the debt increase following 1976 resulted from the efforts to protect our nation from a nuclear attack—in the "Star Wars" program to intercept incoming missile warheads. It became obvious after the May 18, 1980, explosion of Mount St. Helens, (Daniel 2:45:"For as much as thou sawest the stone cut out of the mountain without hands—") that even one 50- or 60-megaton warhead could radioactively cause death over a wide area of our land from fallout residue.

About our overprotective efforts to make our nation invulnerable to attack, the prophecy of Revelation 18:7 that reads in part, "—for she saith in her heart, I sit a queen, and am no widow, and shall see no sorrow" implies just such an attitude and effort.

Since Howard Scott of Technocracy made that prediction in 1946, "In the passing of the old and the instituting of the new, human conflict will become the bitterest in history"—since then we have had the Korean War, the Vietnam War and quantities of CIA/Special Forces interventions in Latin America, Africa, Indonesia, and Vietnam, all to halt the spread of Communism—the "Kingdom of God." The conflict has indeed been bitter!

Before going into the predictions of Edward Bellamy, how our nation might work out our problems, I must mention that there is no indication in the Bible prophecies that this nation did, in fact, work this out—only condemnation of America as Babylon the Great, and the eleventh "little horn" of Daniel 7. Perhaps that is why Edward Bellamy. Thorstein Veblen, Howard Scott, and perhaps myself—were placed here in this time frame as a back-up to save this country from its just desserts. Surely, with this nation's great productive capacity, it could provide great help in uplifting the rest of the world towards their place in "God's Kingdom"—if we would just stop our opposition to it.

In Mark 10:17-27, there is a dialogue between a rich young man, Jesus—and the disciples. The man had kept the commandments from his youth, and Jesus loved him, and told him: 21:"One thing thou lackest, go thy way, sell whatsoever thou hast, and give to the poor—25:It is easier for a camel to go through the eye of a needle, than for a rich man to enter the kingdom of God." I honestly believe that Jesus had shown his disciples the riches of the people of this generation of Americans now living. 26:And they were astonished out of measure, saying among themselves, "Who then can be saved?" 27:And Jesus looking upon them saith, "With men it is impossible, but not with God: For with God all things are possible."

Perhaps this book, and its accurate analysis, will help to accomplish that which seems impossible!!!

In my little "Elton for President" booklet that I had printed in 1976, I quoted pages 340–346 from *Equality*, Bellamy's sequel to *Looking Backward*, to explain some points:

"—The Great Revival was a tide of enthusiasm for the social, not the personal, salvation, and for the establishment in brotherly love of the kingdom of God on earth which Christ bade men hope and work for. It was the general awakening of the people of America in the closing years of the last century to the profoundly ethical and truly religious character and claims of the movement for an industrial system which would guarantee the economic equality of all people.

"Nothing, surely, could be more self-evident than the strictly Christian inspiration of the idea of this guarantee. It contemplated nothing less than a literal fulfillment, on a complete social scale, of Christ's inculcation that all should feel the same solicitude and make the same effort for the welfare of others as for their own. The first effect of such a solicitude must needs be to prompt effort to bring about an equal material provision for all, as the primary condition of welfare. One would certainly think that a nominally Christian people having some familiarity with the New Testament would have needed no one to tell them these things, but that they would have recognized on its first statement that the program of the revolutionists was simply a paraphrase of the golden rule expressed in economic and political terms. One would have said that whatever other members of the community might do, the Christian believers would at once have flocked to the support of such a movement with their whole heart, soul, mind, and might. That they were so slow to do so must be ascribed to the wrong teaching and non-teaching of a class of persons whose express duty, above all others and classes, was to prompt them to that action—namely the Christian clergy.

"For many ages—almost, indeed, from the beginning of the Christian era—the churches had turned their backs on Christ's ideal of a kingdom of God to be realized on earth by the adoption of the law of mutual helpfulness and fraternal love. Giving up the regeneration of human society in this world as a hopeless undertaking, the clergy, in the name of the author of the Lord's Prayer, had taught the people not to expect God's will to be done on earth. Directly reversing the attitude of Christ toward society as an evil and perverse order of things needing to be made over, they had made themselves the bulwarks and defenses of existing social and political institutions, and exerted their whole influence to discourage popular aspirations for a more just and equal order. In the Old World they had been the champions and apologists of power and privilege and vested rights against every movement for freedom and equality. In resisting the upward strivings of their people, the kings and emperors had always found the clergy more useful servants than the soldiers and the police. In the New World, when royalty, in the act of abdication, had passed the scepter behind its back to capitalism, the ecclesiastical bodies had transferred their allegiance to the money power, and as formerly they had preached the divine right of kings to rule their fellowmen, now preached the divine right of ruling and using others which inhered in the possession of accumulated or inherited wealth, and the duty of the people to submit without murmuring to the exclusive appropriation of all good things to the rich.''

(I sincerely believe the above paragraph explains the prophecy of Daniel 9:26:"And after threescore and two weeks shall Messiah be cut off, but not for himself." That would be about A.D. 461.)

"The historical attitude of the churches as the champions and apologists of power and privilege in every controversy with the rights of man and the idea of equality had always been a prodigious scandal, and in every revolutionary crisis had not failed to cost them great losses in public respect and popular following. Inasmuch as the now impending crisis between the full assertion of human equality and the existence of private capitalism was incomparably the most radical issue of the sort that had ever arisen, the attitude of the churches was likely to have a critical effect upon their future. Should they make the mistake of placing themselves upon the unpopular side in this tremendous controversy, it would be for them a colossal if not a fatal mistake—one that would threaten the loss of their hold as organizations on the hearts and minds of the people. On the other hand, had the leaders of the churches been able to discern the full significance of the great turning of the world's heart towards Christ's idea of human society—they might have hoped by taking the right side to rehabilitate the churches in the esteem and respect of the world, as, after all, despite so many mistakes, the faithful representatives of the spirit and doctrine of Christianity. Some there were indeed—yes, many, in the aggregate—among the clergy who did see this and sought desperately to show it to their fellows, but, blinded by the clouds of vain traditions, and bent before the tremendous pressure of capitalism, the ecclesiastical bodies in general did not, with these noble exceptions, awake to their great opportunity until it had passed by. Other bodies of learned men there were which equally failed to discern the irresistible force and divine sanction of the tidal wave of humane enthusiasm that was sweeping over the earth, and to see that it was destined to leave behind it a transformed and regenerated world. But the failure of these others, however lamentable, to discern the nature of the crisis, was not like the failure of the Christian clergy, for it was their express calling and business to preach and teach the application to human relations of the Golden Rule of equal treatment for all which the Revolution came to establish, and to watch for the coming of this very kingdom of brotherly love, whose advent they met with anathemas.

"The reformers of that time were most bitter against the clergy for their double treason to humanity and Christianity, in opposing instead of supporting the Revolution; but time has tempered harsh judgments of every sort, and it is rather with deep pity than with indignation that we look back on these unfortunate men, who will ever retain the tragic distinction of having missed the grandest opportunity of leadership ever offered to men. Why add reproach to the burden of such a failure as that?

"While the influence of ecclesiastical authority in America on account of the growth of intelligence, had at this time greatly shrunken from former proportions, the generally unfavorable or negative attitude of the churches toward the program of equality had told heavily to hold back the popular support which the movement might reasonably have expected from professedly Christian people. It was, however, only a question of time, and the educating influence of public discussion, when the people would become acquainted for themselves with the merits of the subject. *The Great Revival* followed, when, in the course of this process of education, the masses of the nation reached the conviction that the revolution against which the clergy had warned them as unchristian was, in fact, the most essentially and intensely Christian movement that had ever appealed to men since Christ called his disciples, and as such imperatively commanded the strongest support of every believer or admirer of Christ's doctrine.

"The American people appear to have been, on the whole, the most intelligently religious of the large populations of the world—as religion was understood at that time—and the most generally influenced by the sentiment of Christianity. When the people came to recognize that the ideal of a world of equal welfare, which had been represented to them by the clergy as a dangerous delusion, was no other than the very dream of Christ; when they realized that the hope which led on the advocates of the new order was no baleful ignis fatuus, as the churches had taught, but nothing less nor other than the Star of Bethlehem, it is not to be wondered at that the impulse which the revolutionary movement received should have been overwhelming. From that time on it assumes more and more of a crusade, the first of the many so-called crusades of history which had a valid and adequate title to that name and right to make the cross its emblem. As the conviction took hold on the always religious masses that the plan of an equalized human welfare was nothing less than the divine design, and that in seeking their own highest happiness by its adoption they were also fulfilling God's purpose for the race, the spirit of the Revolution became a religious enthusiasm. As to the preaching of Peter the Hermit, so now once more the masses responded to the preaching of the reformers with the exultant cry, 'God wills it!' and none doubted any longer that the vision would come to pass. So it was that the Revolution, which had begun its course under the ban of the churches, was carried to its consummation upon a wave of moral and religious emotion.''

"But what became of the churches and the clergy when the people found out what blind guides they had been?'' I asked.

"No doubt,'' replied the doctor. "It must have seemed to them something like the Judgment Day when their flocks challenged them with open Bibles and demanded why they had hid the Gospel all these ages and falsified the oracles of God which they had claimed to interpret. But so far as appears, the joyous exultation of the people over the discovery that liberty, equality, and fraternity were nothing less than the practical meaning and content of Christ's religion seems to have left them no room in their heart for bitterness toward any class. The world had received a crowning demonstration that was to remain conclusive to all time of the untrustworthiness of ecclesiastical guidance; that was all. The clergy who had failed in their office of guides had not done so, it is needless to say, because they were not as good as other men, but on account of the hopeless falsity of their position as the economic dependents of those they assumed to lead. As soon as the great revival had fairly begun they threw themselves into it as eagerly as any of the people, but not now with any pretensions of leadership. They followed the people whom they might have led.

"From the great revival we date the beginning of the era of modern religion—a religion which had dispensed with the rites and ceremonies, creeds and dogmas, and banished from this life fear and concern for the meaner self; a religion of life and conduct dominated by an impassioned sense of the solidarity of humanity and of man with God; the religion of a race that knows itself divine and fears no evil, either now or hereafter.''

"I need not ask," I said, "as to any subsequent stages of the Revolution, for I fancy its consummation did not tarry long after 'The Great Revival.'"

"That was indeed the culminating impulse," replied the doctor, "but while it lent a momentum to the movement for the immediate realization of an equality of welfare which no obstacle could have resisted, it did its work, in fact, not so much by breaking down opposition as by melting it away. The capitalists, as you who were one of them scarcely need to be told, were not persons of a more depraved disposition than other people, but merely, like other classes, what the economic system made them. Having like passions and sensibilities with other men, they were as incapable of standing out against the contagion of the enthusiasm of humanity, the passion of pity, and the compulsion of humane tenderness which the Great Revival had aroused, as any other class of people. From the time that the sense of the people came generally to recognize that the fight of the existing order was nothing more nor less than a controversy between the almighty dollar and the almighty God, there was substantially but one side to it. A bitter minority of the capitalist party and its supporters seems indeed to have continued its outcry against the Revolution till the end, but it was of little importance. The greater and all the better part of the capitalists joined with the people in completing the installation of the new order which all had come to see was to redound to the benefit of all alike."

"And there was no war?"

"War! Of course not, in a democratic state like America the Revolution was practically done when the people had made up their minds that it was for their interest. There was no one to dispute their power and right to do their will when once resolved on it. The Revolution as regards America and in other countries, in proportion as their governments were popular, was more like the trial of a case in court than a revolution of the traditional blood-and-thunder sort. The court was the people, and the only way that either contestant could win was by convincing the court, from which there was no appeal."

If the above "dream" of Bellamy is to happen, it will require a great deal more interest in the subject on the part of American citizens than has occurred in the past.

The hopes of Bellamy are already nearly a century overdue. The public media erected a "cone of silence" against Technocracy in the early 1930s and have maintained it ever since. With the "merchants" having effective control of the media through advertising revenues, there must needs be some other means of reaching the entire public with the truth of matters. Only time will tell if it can be done, and how.

Besides the correlation of Bible prophecies with events of this twentieth century (which I have publicized for nearly half a century, and which the media, and religionists have largely ignored), I have made an analysis of another matter, which I will elaborate on in the next chapter: The ever-increasing debt of our nation and its people.

IX. Indebtedness—Public and Private

Back in the late 1940s, Technocracy told its members to work and wait; that sometime in the future, the market place would again be glutted with consumer goods and we would again find our nation in the same condition again as in 1929, with a stock market crash and a depression as in the 1930s following. Technocracy proposed to stand by and pick up the pieces by installing a Technocracy—an economy of abundance for all. In their study course, they used graphs to depict the trends of the economy.

In 1962, although I had been out of Technocracy for fourteen years, I had the notion to prepare a graph showing the total public and private indebtedness of our nation and people, and how it related to the federal debt, the population, and unemployment. The graph went back to 1917 when the total debt was only about $95 billion. By 1929 the debt had climbed to $192 billion. It stayed the same in 1930, but it fell off to $170 billion by 1933. Thereafter it climbed slowly to $213 billion by 1941. By 1945 it climbed $195 billion (during World War II) to $408 billion. It fell off a little in 1946 but began climbing again the next year till it had reached $1 trillion by the time I prepared my graph in 1962. The most obvious observation and interpretation of the graph showed that in the early 1930s, when the total debt fell to $170 billion, the unemployment skyrocketed to 21 million unemployed and looking for work, according to the Russell Sage Foundation, which did the research.

From studying the graph that was formed from the figures I got from the *World Almanac and Book of Facts*, I guessed that the total debt would have to increase at an 8 percent compound interest rate per year to keep our economy healthy and progressing.

The graph was seventeen centimeters high, and each centimeter represented $60 billion debt. The graph at the time fitted neatly on an 8½-by-11 inch page of typewriter paper, with the $1 trillion spot almost reaching the top of the graph. I made copies of it and added an explanation of what it all meant. Since I had been interested in the millennium, or millennial age, I wondered how it would all work out, doubling our total debt for a number of years—or a thousand years in a millennium. At 8 percent compounded annually, the amount of debt would double about every ten years; $2 trillion by 1972, $4 trillion by 1982, $8 trillion by 1992, $16 trillion by 2002, $32 trillion by 2012, $64 trillion by 2022, etc.

Actually, the total debt climbed at a near 10 percent per annum rate between 1962 and 1976, when it reached $3.37 trillion that year and federal debt portion was up to $554 billion in 1976, or roughly one-sixth of the total.

If the total federal debt and private were calculated on a ratio of one to six (1:6), then the total debt probably rose to over $30 trillion by 1996 when the federal debt had risen to over $5 trillion.

Actually, a 10 percent per annum increase in the total debt would have only raised it to about $22½ trillion by 1996, so two different conclusions might be drawn from this nearly $10 trillion difference. One: perhaps the federal debt increase amounted to a greater than one-sixth share of the total. Two: perhaps the total debt is continually increasing at an ever faster rate.

I must mention one fact. Following my presentation of my graph in a full page ad in the *Medford Mail Tribune*, May 17, 1976, the government stopped calculating the total debt in their annual reports, so one can only guess at the true figures for the total debt.

Another conclusion that might be drawn from the above figures: perhaps the increase in the federal debt is of a higher percentage of the total debt during the 1976–1996 period of time, and amounted to a pump-priming of the economy that is still supporting it long after the infusion took place.

At this stage of my dissertation, I should try to list some of the various debts that we are talking about.

Of course, on the public debt side, we must first off list the federal debt, now close to $5.5 trillion. Then there are school bonds, municipal debt, and some states are in debt to lenders, etc.

In the private sector, one can list home mortgage debt, credit debt, time payment plans for furniture, household appliances, and personal loans, and start-up loans for small businesses, etc.

One kind of debt that must be considered is corporate debt, the value of the stocks traded on the various stock exchanges; Dow Jones, NASDAQ, American Stock exchange, etc. When one buys a share of stock, one expects a good return on the investment, either in dividends paid to the stockholder periodically, and/or through increased value of the share of stock. Sometimes some of the profit for a period may be turned back into new equipment and production facilities, and this would increase the total value of the holdings, and would be reflected in a rise of the value of the stock on the exchange—as well as the dividend rate of return on the share of stock.

The point I make is that every debt is expected to return a good percentage rate of return, per dollar invested, or loaned.

Some debts are at a fixed rate for given period of time. Most home loans, CDs, etc., are of that nature. Shares of stock are more flexible, subject to the ups and downs of the economy. If a share of stock does not continue to increase in value, or the divided results are skimpy, or both, the value of a stock will prove to be a poor investment and the stock will be sold, further depressing the value as and when many investors decide also to sell for the same reasons.

So individually, and in aggregate, the stock holders demand that the corporation make a profit—or else. The managers (CEOs, etc.) do what they have to to make a profit and issue dividends to encourage stock holders to hold onto their shares, and/or buy more. The purchase of a share of stock is in fact a loan of the price of the stock to the corporation that issued the stock, therefore a private debt of the corporation.

There is one aspect of this increase of private indebtedness that needs to be considered—the inflated property values over the past fifty or sixty years. In mid-1941, I purchased a two-bedroom house with double garage attached on Hammack Street in a western section of Culver City, California, just a few blocks from where Howard Hughes built a factory, for $3,150. If that house were still there, it would probably now sell for $100,000 to $150,000, or thirty to fifty times what I purchased it for. The three-bedroom houses in the tract sold for a little more—$3,750 in 1941.

Wages have risen since 1941, markedly, but I believe housing costs have increased even faster. Perhaps that is one reason why there are so many homeless people around the country at present.

But back to the thousand-year millennial age that is supposed to lie ahead of us. If our economy depends on an ever-increasing debt to remain "healthy," and it does appear to be increasing at an ever larger annual percentage rate as well, perhaps nearing 15 percent at present, what might happen as the years go by?

Early on I calculated the amount the debt would become near the end of a thousand years at 8 percent increase annually. The figure came to $4, followed by some 47 digits before the decimal point. If the whole mass of the earth were pure gold at the 1962 rate of $32/oz, it would not begin to equal the total debt at the end of a thousand years.

On the shorter term, beginning at $1 trillion in 1962, and doubling every ten years, by 2062, it would equal $512 trillion; by 2162 it would equal $262,144 trillion; by 2262 it would equal $134,219,728 trillion.

The point I am trying to make is that, with our economy depending on the necessary debt increase indicated by a careful analysis of my graph, drawn from actual figures, to remain healthy, it cannot be an effective means of advance into the distant future.

In a Technocracy there would be no debt. The economy could be geared to the consumption needs and desires of the population, and through continuous flow monitoring of the consumption, the production facilities could be kept producing at the rate indicated by the purchasing public. Computers can do wonders when programmed to do so.

In both Edward Bellamy's ideal and Technocracy's design, there would be no money or medium of exchange involved. The "state" would issue an amount of energy units or dollars to each one's account each year, or two, and any left over at the end of two years would revert back to the state, and a new allotment would be issued for the next time period. The transactions would be between the state and the individual by way of credit card or its equivalent, without any interest charged or indicated. We can produce such an abundance of everything that no one would come up short of anything. Without any medium of exchange, very likely this arrangement would eliminate the drug traffic completely, and any other black market activities.

One last thought on the corporate debt; just the other day I received a circular called the *Fleet Street Letter*, in which they stated that the value of stocks had risen from $1 trillion in 1982 to some $10 trillion by the time of its writing. In the crash of 1987, less than eleven years ago, the Dow was down to a little over 1700 points; it is now well over 9000 points as of this writing.

You can find Edward Bellamy's books, *Equality and Looking Backward*—2000–1887 A.D. by requesting them at almost any public library; and perhaps Technocracy is still around to find out from its current leadership what can be done.

Parade Magazine, a Sunday supplement, for April 19, 1998, had an article about the future, with some quotes from famous people, and "Edward Bellamy—a novelist—was the most farsighted of all. In his 1888 novel *Looking Backward—2000–1887*, he described an "American Credit card, just as good in Europe as American gold used to be." And seven years before Marconi demonstrated the first commercial use of radio, Bellamy wrote, "Our bed chambers have (an) attachment to the head of the bed by which any person who may be sleepless can command music at pleasure." He even foreshadowed the women's movement. "A woman does not necessarily leave the industrial service on marriage no more than a man," wrote Bellamy. "Why on earth should she?"

Summary

In essence, this book is a classic murder mystery, in most respects much like *Perry Mason*, Matlock, *Murder She Wrote*, or *Diagnosis Murder*. In a *Matlock* or *Perry Mason* thriller, the evidence seems to be overwhelmingly against the accused. In our twentieth century case, the Communists are accused of the murder(s) in the minds of the bulk of the American people, thanks to articles like appeared regularly in one of America's most read magazines, *Reader's Digest*. Typical is an article in the April 1996 issue, quoting an article by Jeff Jacoby in the *Boston Globe*, headlined "To the Victims of Communism—Lest We Forget." To quote in part, "The Nazis exterminated 11 million innocents, and while the Holocaust was uniquely malignant, the Communist death toll surpasses 100 million." (I don't suppose, in the eyes of Jacoby and *Reader's Digest* that the 28 million Russians, soldiers and civilians, that the German and West European invasion forces killed in their war of aggression against the USSR were considered "innocents.")

Reader's Digest brags about checking the facts of their articles, but I suppose if someone else makes certain statements, they can be reported as such without checking the facts.

I am not suggesting that the Communists did not kill anyone—only that the numbers are grossly exaggerated—and anyhow Jesus clearly explained what might be necessary in his parable of the pounds in Luke 19:11–27. The last paragraph clearly states (27): "But those mine enemies, which would not that I should reign over them, bring hither, and slay them before me,'' in relation to the setting up the Kingdom of God on the earth.

The Bible prophecy, of John, Revelation 17:5—who is Babylon the Great, constitutes the one (1) mystery, explicitly stated. But in reality, there is another mystery: "Who are the good guys—and who are the bad guys, in this twentieth century—end times?"

The American people, I sincerely believe, would have recognized the answer to that last question long ago, if only the news media would have allowed the findings of the Bertrand Russell (Ancient of Days) War Tribunal teams to be considered by all Americans. That is the reason why I included so much of those findings in this book. But the politicians who have presided over our Cold War and Vietnam War policies, have been subservient to the rich men who pass out the campaign funds; and the media are subservient to the advertisers who pay the costs of news dissemination—the merchants, "The Great Men of the Earth."

Hundreds of years before Jesus was born and served his ministry, Daniel received word that in the days of certain kings, of the fourth beast, that the God of heaven would set up a kingdom on earth (Daniel 2:44). In Daniel 7, in three descriptions, it tells of these kings, how they would go out to conquer the whole earth and stomp, tread down, etc., the residue thereof. Some religionists (really false prophets) point to the European Common Market nations as that potential for that action. They have to be totally wrong—the European nations that explored, conquered, and colonized following Columbus's voyages and discovery of the New World, completely fit that picture.

The treatment of the Native Americans by the European colonists who came here to settle, probably exemplifies the treatment of the indigenous peoples most of all. I read not long ago of an estimate that there were 15 million or more Native Americans here when Europeans arrived, and by the end of the "Indian" wars in the 1800s, their numbers had been reduced to less than one million—as they were killed, deprived of their lands, and sent to reservations (concentration camps).

The Daniel 7 prophecy also tells of an eleventh nation (little horn) that would rise up and would subdue three, and thereafter "speak great words against the most High, and shall wear out the saints of the most High—" Since the United States was primarily colonized by European nations and peoples, the USA has to be the "little horn" of Daniel 7, in view also of our participation in the battle against all *three* major Axis-Pact-of-Fascism powers of World War II.

The Cold War began about April 22, 1945, even before the German armies had surrendered, according to two historians, D. F. Fleming of Vanderbilt University in his book *The Cold War and Its Origins*, and according to Fred Cook in *The Warfare State*, in which he described the ongoing policies of our nation up to the early 1960s. Daniel 7 and also Daniel 12 refer to a time, times, and the dividing of time (3½ times), which takes matters up to October 22, 1962, if a time represents five years—to the Cuban Missile Crisis, which was far more serious than most Americans realized. Most of the political leaders in the Vietnam War era, have gone the way of all flesh, just as has Bertrand Russell (Ancient of Days of Daniel 7) the "one like unto the Son of man" in Daniel 7 and Revelation 14 (Lenin); and the "Lamb" of Revelation 14:and 17:(Joseph Stalin) who held two positions of power in the Soviet Union. First or General Secretary of the Communist Party in the USSR and Premier of the Union of Socialist Soviet Republics, or as the Bible calls it, "Lord of Lords and King of Kings."

The "saints of the most High" of Daniel 7 and that 144,000, first redeemed to God and the Lamb, who; would follow the Lamb whither-so-ever he goest of Revelation 14:"and those that were with Him were called, chosen and faithful'' of Revelation 17:comprised the Communist leadership of the Soviet Union in World War II. The beast (Hitler) and ten "Quisling" leaders who would give their power and strength to the beast for *one hour*—the Fascist-minded leaders whom Hitler put in charge after he conquered practically all of Europe—all under approval of the "rich men" of Europe—made their attack upon the Soviet Union in June of 1941.

Robert McNamara, who orchestrated much of America's aggression against little Vietnam as Secretary of Defense (offense), is still around, although retired, and he redeemed himself somewhat on two occasions. One, when he ordered the Defense Department to compile a history of our involvement in Vietnam, which became known as the "Pentagon Papers" when publicized in 1971, before he resigned his defense position in 1968. Two, when he wrote his book on the war, *In Retrospect*, and included an epilogue at the end telling just how serious the Cuban Missile Crisis really was. He reported that if an agreement had not been reached by the time it did, our invasion forces were ready on Monday to invade Cuba. It was found out later, according to McNamara, that there were quantities of *tactical nuclear weapons* already there, ready to be used against any troop invasion—which would have probably escalated to an all-out nuclear war.

Hence, the "abomination of desolation standing where it ought not," of Mark 13:14 was indeed the Cuban Missile Crisis. The danger that no (human) flesh would be saved if it had gone to its climax, was very real. Look it up in Mark 13:14–32.

Now about Babylon the Great: I related my analysis of America's responsibility for so much bloodshed and death, as the Bible blames Babylon the Great for in my 1980 letter to Pres. Carter, which was refused publication in *Talent Magazine*, when five previous ads had been accepted—and "Mother Nature's" response three days after I gave up. Mount St. Helens—"the stone cut out of the mountain without hands'' (Daniel 2:45) and a dramatic demonstration of the area covered by deadly fall-out, should it have been one of Russia's fifty-megaton explosive devices.

But let's look at some more evidence that describes Babylon the Great in Revelation 16, 17, and 18. In 17:5 it says "Mother of harlots and Abominations of the earth.'' The latter points to the atomic and nuclear bombs, which America definitely was the mother of. The "harlots'' are the nations and their leaders that have lined up behind America's anti-Communist efforts—especially the NATO nations (most of which were co-invaders of the Soviet Union with Hitler in 1941) and the Pacific Rim countries that have recently fallen into financial difficulties, some of which assisted the U.S. against the people of Vietnam. Then there are some Latin American nations where our CIA and Special Forces helped to get a "Friendly to America'' regime established, either by overthrow of the previous government, or assistance to friendly regimes.

Revelation 18:3:"For all nations have drunk of the wine of the wrath of her fornication, and the kings of the earth have committed fornication with her, and the merchants of the earth are waxed rich through the *abundance* of her delicacies.''

There are more descriptions that definitely fit the America of this twentieth century; and the bulk of the chapter deals with what might happen to her; and it isn't pretty.

In studying this prophecy, the first thought that struck me was that a nuclear war would destroy America—on the basis of the suddenness that it could happen (in one hour) and on the description of the smoke of her burning rising up forever and ever, in Revelation 19:3. (The principle of nuclear radiation having a half-life, after so many years only half as much radiation from the fall-out; etc.)

Then more recently I have thought of the Revelation 16:18–19 and 18:21 description indicating an asteroid or comet hit—like in the made-for-TV movie *Asteroid*. In the movie parts of the asteroid fell all over the earth after it had been broken up by laser beams.

Another serious possibility is the total public and private debt problem reaching such huge figures that the whole economy might collapse, as it did in 1929 and through the early 1930s. Hardly a month passes by that I don't receive a warning from some financial experts like the *Fleet Street Letter*, *Wall Street Underground*, *Strategic Investment*, etc., predicting the crash and offering advice on how to survive the crash, and in fact prosper—if I would just subscribe to their newsletter.

I have no idea how soon that crash will come, but it is obvious that at some point the debt level of our nation and people, increasing at an 8 to 15 percent annual rate of increase, will get so high that the situation will become overwhelming. At present the Federal Reserve Board and the administration are carefully managing things to prevent such a collapse soon.

Then just the other day I received a circular from Dr. Gary North's *Remnant Review* expressing concern for the year 2000 bug that might affect computer programs for Social Security, banks, and other aspects of our society that depend on computer data. Of course all these warnings are intended to promote membership in their particular newsletter.

Perhaps these dangers are like the sword of Damocles hanging by a thread over our nation because of its wrong course and misdeeds over the past years. Perhaps we should "post-haste" adopt the ideals described by Edward Bellamy describing the year 2000 society, and improved on as to application by Thorstein Veblen and Howard Scott in the Technocracy program, and most of all stop opposing communism, "The Kingdom of God," in the rest of the world.

There are two guidelines in the Scriptures for the "rich men" of today. One is the advice of Jesus to the "rich man" in Mark 10:18–24, and the other in the response of two of the servants in the parable of the pounds, as opposed to the other 7 or 8 in Luke 19:11–27.

On my birthday, February 10, 1966, I prepared a paper on my then most recent analysis of the prophecies, and along with it several pages of "The War" in Vietnam. At the end of one page, I listed a few references from the Bible: Matthew 16:1–4, and Luke 11:29–36. In the latter, these were the words of Jesus to people who were gathered together:

> —This is an evil generation: they seek a sign; and there shall no sign be given it, but the sign of Jonas the prophet: 30 For as Jonas was a sign unto the Ninevites, so shall also the Son of man be to this generation. 31 The queen of the south shall rise up in judgment with the men of this generation, and condemn them; for she came from the utmost parts of the earth to hear the wisdom of Solomon, and behold a greater than Solomon is here. 32 The men of Nineveh shall rise up in the judgment with this generation, and shall condemn it; for they repented at the preaching of Jonas, and behold a greater than Jonas is here.

I wonder if that thought is not even more appropriate for the people of this century, and this nation.

About the wisdom of Solomon, I remember one decision that he arrived at after hearing both sides of a case in which two women each claimed that a certain baby was hers alone. After hearing the arguments, he offered to cut the baby in half and give half to each. The false mother agreed, but the real mother knew that would kill the baby and said no—let her have the baby, and thus Solomon knew how to decide.

A similar decision on the part of the Russians and Chinese may have been reached over the past decade or so. The Cold War confrontation had been going on for nearly half a century, the last two-thirds of that time any nuclear war would have destroyed all human life on this earth; and then who would have been here to finish establishing God's everlasting kingdom on earth, as Christians have been praying for for nearly two thousand years—"Thy kingdom come, Thy will be done in (on) earth as it is in heaven." So the Communists backed off—perhaps thinking, "If we can't beat them (safely), we might as well join them."

The managers of our production and distribution facilities could be very useful in developing the ideals of Edward Bellamy's visions, as further expanded on by Thorstein Veblen and in Howard Scott's Technocracy.

Addendum 1: Guatemala

A news item in the *Medford Mail Tribune* for February 26, 1999, headlined "Guatemala Hears Truth", tells that the Guatemalan army is responsible for the vast majority of the more than 200,000 deaths and disappearances in the country's 36-year civil war.

The long awaited report, based on the testimony of 9,200 people from all sides in the conflict, was Guatemala's first step in bringing reconcillation to a country split since a U.S.-backed coup put rightists in power in 1954.

Of the 42,000 deaths investigated in the report, the army was found to be responsible for 93 percent. The report found that 29,000 of the investigated deaths involved summary executions.

Most of the victims were civilians and Mayan Indians.

The report also noted that "the government of the United States, through various agencies, including the CIA, provided direct and indirect support for some state operations."

The U.N.'s truth commission's members, appointed as part of the 1996 peace accords, investigated atrocities committed during a war that pitted leftist rebels against the army and paramilitary death squads.

It was "clearly genocide and a planned strategy against the civilian population," said Christian Tomuschat, a German citizen who heads the three member commission.

In 626 massacres, the report found that government forces "completely exterminated Mayan communities, destroyed their dwellings, livestock and crops." The guerrillas were blamed for only 32 such massacres, the report said.

Army officials have said the massacres were excesses on the part of individual officers. (Officers who were trained at the school of the Americas in Panama—by the U.S. army???)

Not long after the above item appeared in the newspaper, President Clinton made a special trip to Guatemala and apologized to their nation for America's part in the killings, and also promised to send monetary help to them to help recover from the hurricane damage they suffered last year.

Addendum 2: Kosovo

From 1954 to 1964, "North" Vietnam made great strides under Ho Chi Minh in reducing illiteracy, building schools, health facilities, etc., and generally improving the lot of the people. And then came the fake Tonkin Gulf incident.

Was that the reason that America elected to bomb them, destroying the progress they had made under a Communist leadership; bombing schools, churches, hospitals, dikes and villages brutally?

Yugoslavia likewise has made good progress in improving the lot of their people under a socialist-Communist leadership, and is the last Communist-led nation in Europe. President Clinton sent his dear friend and Secretary of Commerce, Ron Brown, over there to recruit some capitalist-inclined managers a few years ago—and they were all killed in a pilot-error crash while attempting to land. Is Clinton subconsciously blaming Yugoslavia for the loss of his friend? "Mother Nature" as well had a hand in that crash.

Earlier this decade there were some Kosovars that were considered terrorists and drug smugglers. Somebody changed their purpose in life to that of a Kosovar Liberation Army, dedicated to gaining independence from Yugoslavia. Was it our CIA that thereby stirred up the current crisis in Kosovo—to develop an excuse to destroy the last Communist-led nation and bomb it back into the stone age, as Lyndon Johnson and Richard Nixon did to North Vietnam?

Some of the NATO nations assisted Hitler to conquering Yugoslavia at the outset of World War II. Is it any wonder that

Milosevic objects to NATO troops occupying a part of his nation? As for the refugees from Kosovo, I don't believe their cause has been helped a bit by the bombings. The only thing accomplished is a vast destruction of a hated (by the rich men of today) Communist-led country that might prove successful for the improvement of their people.

Perhaps "Mother Nature" disapproves as well of America's cause célèbre, as witness the devastation inflicted on the center of our nation on May 3, 1999.